A different kind of cookbook, from a different kind of restaurant. The team behind the award-winning Montreal pizza joint Elena presents *Salad Pizza Wine*, delivering recipes for all of life's good things, with fresh, delicious and easy-to-recreate takes on modern Italian dishes, including:

Elena's famous pizza

If you could eat pizza every day and feel great, would you believe it? From heavy-hitters to off-menu pies, the secret to a pizza-filled life is in Elena's naturally leavened dough.

Salads + Vegetables

Like people, this book contains multitudes; you can stuff your face with pizza on the daily and take pleasure in eating vegetables with the seasons.

Pasta

Learn how to make two super versatile doughs and their multiple variations, and impress your loved ones with an all-star roster of favorite pastas.

Meat + Fish

Take your pick from weeknight-friendly recipes, dishes to save for special occasions and one once-in-a-lifetime adventure: the gargantuan Timpano, inspired by the classic film *Big Night*.

Hoagies

Who doesn't love sandwiches? Portable and easy to share with a friend, hoagies are also perfect for wrapping up all your tasty leftovers.

Desserts

End every meal on a high note with a series of serious sweet treats for beginners and advanced bakers alike.

Go-Tos

Lay the foundation for your home-cooking adventure with basic recipes that deliver big flavor, from crunchy toasted breadcrumbs and multi-purpose sauces to simple pickles and homemade cheeses.

More than a collection of recipes, *Salad Pizza Wine* shares Elena's passion for natural wines too—the wine part of *Salad Pizza Wine*—as well as their goofs and thoughts on living a fuller life. The authors—Janice, Stephanie, Ryan, Marley—were part of Elena's opening team who came together, burnt out from years in the restaurant industry and ready to start afresh. Their answer was to create a restaurant that was also a healthy working environment (gasp). At Elena, it's all about making the most of a good thing—and the same goes for this book. Whether it's planning a dinner (salad, pizza, wine? pizza, pasta, dessert? salad, meat, hoagie?), or letting go of stuff that no longer serves you, *Salad Pizza Wine* encourages you to choose your own adventure—both in the kitchen and in life.

Written in a self-deprecating, tongue-in-cheek style, this is a cookbook you'll really want to cook from, as well as to read. Because what's better than cooking beautiful food, being kind to those around us and laughing as we all try to figure it out?

COFFEE PIZZA WINE
SERVICE AU COMPTOI
BAROLO
ARBOIS PUPILLIN
DE FERMO
La capitulation
NE PAIE PAS!
DONATI CAMILLO
La Villana
ORSI

SALAD

PIZZA

WINE

and many more good things from Elena

By Janice Tiefenbach, Stephanie Mercier Voyer,
Ryan Gray and Marley Sniatowsky

appetite
BY RANDOM HOUSE

Appetite by Random House® and colophon are registered
trademarks of Penguin Random House LLC.

Library and Archives Canada Cataloguing in Publication is
available upon request.
ISBN: 978-0-52-561177-6
eBook ISBN: 978-0-52-561178-3

Photography by Dominique Lafond
Photography styling by Elisabeth Racine
Illustrations by Emilie Campbell
Cover and book design by Jennifer Griffiths
Recipe testing by Michelle Marek and Kendra McKnight
Printed in China

Published in Canada by Appetite by Random House®,
a division of Penguin Random House Canada Limited

www.penguinrandomhouse.ca

10 9 8 7 6 5 4 3 2 1

appetite
by RANDOM HOUSE

TO OUR STAFF,
PAST AND PRESENT.

CONTENTS

INTRO

by

Stephanie Mercier Voyer

Ryan Gray is one of the first people I called when my life fell apart in 2017. We'd met a few years earlier when he hired me to work at his first restaurant, Nora Gray, and once again, I needed a job. He was about to open a new spot called Elena with partners Emma Cardarelli and Marley Sniatowsky. Chef Janice Tiefenbach, who had also worked at Nora Gray, would helm the kitchen. Ryan offered me a server position on the spot.

When Nora Gray opened in 2011, Italian food in Montreal was synonymous with checkered-tablecloth, Italian American red-sauce joints. Nora was everything but. Emma's cooking explored regionally specific Italian dishes using fresh ingredients from Quebec, while Ryan's wine list introduced the city's palate to some of the most remarkable natural winemakers. Nora Gray is where I truly fell in love with food and wine. It was and remains one of the best tables in town.

Opening a more casual restaurant focused on wood-fire pizza and natural wine felt like the natural progression to what Nora Gray had started. By 2017, natural wine had carved its way onto several wine lists across Montreal, but no one in the city was making local, seasonal pizza. They wanted to change that with Elena. The wisdom at the time was that to make the best, most authentic Neapolitan pizza, you had to import everything from Italy, from the oven to the flour, tomatoes and even the water. But the thing that makes Neapolitan pizza so delicious and unique is that all the ingredients are fresh and sourced locally. Italian cuisine is all about using what can be found in your specific region. That's why Northern Italian pasta receives a shower of Parmigiano-Reggiano, while Central Italian dishes are sprinkled with pecorino. Naturally, opening a restaurant that made Neapolitan pizza using Quebec ingredients felt more authentically Italian than making dough with imported 00 flour and bottled water from Naples.

When I showed up in Montreal, a week after my phone call with Ryan, to visit an apartment in St-Henri, a neighborhood that at the time felt eons away from the bustle of the city, I ran into Marley. He was covered in construction dust and had a big smile on his face. He asked if I wanted to come check out the building across the street. Tucked between a boarded-up apartment building and a dépanneur, this unassuming, brown-bricked storefront would soon house Elena. There was no floor, no staircase, no ceiling and no electricity. "This is where the open kitchen is going to be—openness is what this place is all about," gestured Marley as we walked over generators and construction lamps. "Oh, and we're building a massive wood-fire oven over there. And that's where we're going to

set up the pizza slide." The twinkle in his eye registered as someone who was both excited and completely insane.

That night, a bunch of our friends (people who would end up being part of Elena's opening crew) gathered at Marley's for dinner. All of us came of age working in the restaurant industry at a time when excess was akin to greatness. We had seen and done it all: late nights, drugs, alcohol, yelling and getting into fights. But now that we were older, we felt kind of burnt out. We were ready for a new chapter and we were hoping that new chapter could be Elena.

During dinner, dough wizard Jake "Bigsby" Bagshaw talked about the intricacies of the perfect pizza and Ryan yapped about bringing natural wine to the masses with a program that featured winemakers who shared our ethos. Elena the restaurant, he explained, was even named after one of those winemakers, the legendary Elena Pantaleoni from La Stoppa in Emilia-Romagna. She represented everything we aspired to be. Throughout her career, Elena has pushed against the grain, making decisions that were financially risky but that she knew would benefit the planet and her community in the long run. Inspired to break the mold, we all chimed in about the kind of place we wanted Elena to be. "Any idiot can open a restaurant," laughed Marley while pointing at us. "Some people can open a great restaurant, but very few people can open a restaurant that's also a healthy environment."

That's what we set out to do at Elena—to create a place where people could feel safe to express who they are, try things and become their better selves. We were aware of the risks of doing things differently and putting people's well-being ahead of business objectives. But we

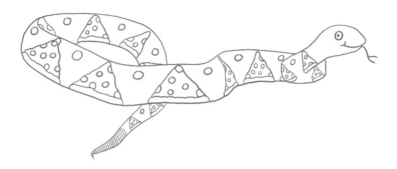

knew in our guts that this was the only way we'd survive as people.

We had to burn it all down and start from scratch. Ryan often says that restaurants, just like people, have their own DNA, a set of unique qualities that are determined before birth. Let's say you open a restaurant where you push your staff to their limits with long hours and verbal abuse, then reward them with copious amounts of alcohol. It becomes extremely hard to change that kind of culture later on. It's in the restaurant's DNA. But there are steps you can take from the beginning that will have a positive impact on your restaurant's evolution.

It was in Elena's colorful and slick Italian modern dining room designed by our friend Kyle Adams Goforth that we allowed ourselves to dream of something better, and experiment with food, wine and interpersonal relationships. In the kitchen, Janice set the tone by leading with kindness, de facto becoming the antithesis of the cartoonishly angry bro-chef. Staff were given shorter work weeks than in most restaurants to encourage a healthier work-life balance, and also subsidized healthcare. And unlike at most

restaurants, we never stayed for more than a single drink after our shifts. We mostly wanted to go to bed early to hit the rock-climbing gym in the morning. There was friction, of course, and adjustments had, and continue, to be made. Nothing in life is perfect or ever will be. But slowly we started to feel at ease—happy, even. We could breathe better.

Ryan explained this shift to me over coffee one morning. "We don't need to perform anymore," he said. "Everything we do now comes from a place of generosity instead of always trying to compensate for our insecurities." This is something we've continued to do at Elena and at our newest spot Gia, an Italian grill restaurant we opened in part to give the team even more opportunity to grow as individuals and professionals.

Salad Pizza Wine (a take on Elena's tagline "Coffee Pizza Wine") is as much about the recipes as it is about sharing some goofs and thoughts on creating a fuller life for yourself while taking care of the people around you. This is a somewhat wholesome book from people who are still trying to figure out what it's like to feel whole. We hope our recipes and stories make you feel like you are allowed to reimagine your life and choose your own adventure. Whether it's letting go of stuff that's no longer helping you or planning a dinner menu that looks something like Salad Pizza Wine, Pizza Pasta Dessert or Salad Meat Hoagie, it's all up to you.

ABOUT THIS BOOK

Choosing your own adventure is a concept we've been obsessed with since before we opened Elena, and we refer to it a bunch in the pages of this book. At the restaurant, choosing your own adventure means that we offer people the option to eat inside or outside, upstairs or downstairs, and even take out. Elena, and how you choose to enjoy it, contains multitudes. You can come for coffee and a hoagie with your parents during the day and then come back later in the evening on a first date for some pizza and wine. It's about making the most of a good thing.

We've divided this book into seven chapters not only to reflect the way we've historically laid out the menu at Elena, but also to allow you to mix and match recipes from different chapters to create one-of-a-kind meals (read: your own adventure).

First up is the Salads + Vegetables chapter. While we could stuff our face with pizza every day (and we do), we also love eating our vegetables

with the seasons. Since we're always working on a million different projects, it's easy for us to feel disconnected and like time is something that just happens to us. Eating vegetables when they're in their prime (whether it's a savory beefsteak tomato in August or a blush-pink radicchio in the winter) is a good way to stay connected with what's happening around us. It's also allowed us to build friendships with some of the people who grow our food, and what's more fun than friends?

There's the Pizza chapter, honoring one of the most perfect foods ever created. If we were to tell our younger selves that we'd grow up to eat pizza every day *and* feel great, they wouldn't believe us. ("Listen to me, kid. In the future, natural fermentation is a game changer for us.") In this chapter, you will find a combination of Elena heavy hitters, sleeper hits and off-menu items you probably didn't even know existed. Pro tip: use recipes from chapters 1 and 2 to craft a glorious menu for your next pizza party.

The Pasta chapter teaches you the basics of pasta making with two super-versatile basic doughs (semolina dough and egg dough). We also spill the tea on our all-time favorite pasta dishes, some of which are perfect for pasta-curious cooks while others are more suited for advanced pasta lovers looking for a challenge (ahem, Raviolo Giardino).

Up next is the Meat + Fish chapter, which lays out recipes you will want to make throughout the week (Dante Chicken Thighs are a great

example), dishes to save for special events (think Porchetta with Peach Mostarda) and once-in-a-lifetime adventures like a gargantuan Timpano, inspired by the classic film *Big Night*.

Hoagies are great because they're portable and easy to share with a friend, and they've essentially saved our restaurant (more on that later). What's especially great about the hoagies in this book is that a lot of them can be made using leftovers from other recipes. And if you know us, you know we hate wasting food.

A lot of restaurants treat desserts as an afterthought, with savory items and wine being the main event (we've been guilty of that in the past). But now that we are older and our sweet tooth has completely gone off the rails, we see things differently. That is why we packed the Desserts chapter with some of our favorite sweet treats to ensure you end every meal on the highest note possible.

Think of the final chapter of our book, Our Go-Tos, as the field guide to your adventure. It's a great reference with basic recipes that we use throughout the book, from crunchy toasted breadcrumbs and multi-purpose sauces to simple pickles and homemade cheeses.

Choosing your own adventure is all about giving you the opportunity to figure out what you like, inside and outside the kitchen. Obviously, this book is full of recipes with clear and detailed instructions to follow, but ultimately you are the one in charge here. If there's an ingredient you just can't stand, feel free to skip it or replace it with something else whenever it makes sense. Same goes for the amount of seasoning called for in any of our recipes, which is why we will repeat time and again to taste and adjust to your liking. Many of our ingredient lists will empower you to choose different varieties of a given vegetable. We also encourage you to try different shapes and colors because, just like choosing your own adventure, cooking should be fun.

INGREDIENTS ARE EVERYTHING

You've heard it before, but we will say it again: great ingredients make all the difference. Skills and technique can't hurt, but quality ingredients will effectively bridge the gap between a good meal and a lights-out culinary experience. We suggest you try to buy organic ingredients as much as possible because what's good for you is also good for the planet. Here, we list a few of the staples you'll want to stock up on to cook from this book or just to be ready for whatever life throws at you, whether that's a last-minute dinner with friends or a global pandemic.

Salt
Salt is life. We always have two different types of salt in the kitchen, kosher salt and flaky sea salt. We like to cook with kosher salt and finish our dishes with a pinch of nice flaky sea salt. All the recipes in this book that use kosher salt have been tested using Diamond Crystal's fine kosher salt (the main exception is our pizza dough, which we make with fine sea salt). You can use another brand of kosher salt or even sea salt to make any of the dishes in this book, but keep in mind that not all salt is created equal. This means you might have to adjust the amount of salt that you use (for example, Morton's kosher salt is about twice as salty as Diamond Crystal's). For flaky sea salt, we love fleur de sel, but Maldon is also good—as long as you find a flaky sea salt that has a nice crunch to it. Finishing salt is all about adding an extra layer of texture to the dish.

Black pepper
We always use whole black peppercorns and grind them only when needed for optimal freshness. Pre-ground black pepper generally lacks flavor.

Extra virgin olive oil
We can't stress enough the importance of cooking with good-quality extra virgin olive oil. Like we do with salt, we prefer to use two different kinds of olive oil in the kitchen. We cook with a more affordable olive oil and use a more expensive, higher-quality oil for finishing touches. We like to get frivolous with our finishing olive oil and buy it from winemakers we love, like Pacina and La Villana. In both cases, try to find a single-origin olive oil so that you know there are no additives or fillers involved.

Vegetable oil
Some people like to use olive oil for everything, which is great, but it can get pretty expensive. If you know you're going to use a lot of oil for a recipe (i.e., if you're frying suppli or eggplant), we recommend using a flavor-neutral vegetable oil like sunflower or grapeseed.

Vinegars

We love vinegars of all kinds because they can brighten up a salad or a sauce in a flash. Stock up your pantry with red wine vinegar, white wine vinegar, sherry vinegar, natural cider vinegar and balsamic, and you should be good to go. If you can, try buying naturally brewed vinegars made without synthetic ingredients.

Canned tomatoes

Cooking with good-quality canned tomatoes is crucial, and when it comes to pizza, the best advice we can give is to keep things as simple as possible. Passata, whole, crushed, peeled or diced—it doesn't really matter as long as the tomatoes are high quality and preferably low salt. Look for Italian D.O.P. (Denominazione di Origine Protetta) products or organic North American brands like Bianco DiNapoli (a collaboration between pizza guru Chris Bianco and third-generation canner Rob DiNapoli). We like to sauce our pizzas with Bianco DiNapoli crushed tomatoes straight out of the can because they are already incredibly delicious, have a nice consistency and contain just a touch of salt. But the truth is, there is no right or wrong answer when it comes to choosing which brand of canned tomatoes to use. It really comes down to what *you* like. If all you have on hand are whole peeled tomatoes, you can break them by hand for a chunkier sauce, pass them through a food mill or pulse for a few seconds in a food processor. The only thing we don't recommend is using a blender to crush your tomatoes. High-speed blending tends to introduce a lot of air, which will alter the flavor and consistency of the tomato sauce and make it too smooth.

Flour

Flour is so important when it comes to making pizza dough, bread and pasta. For our pizzas and pastas, we use all-purpose, whole wheat,

bread, spelt and semolina rimacinata (perfect to make semolina pasta dough and to dust your work surface when working with different kinds of dough) flours. Try to buy flour that is freshly milled locally whenever you can. The reason is simple. As soon as whole wheat flour is milled, the oil contained in the wheat begins to oxidize, resulting in a significant loss of flavors and aromas after some time.

Fresh mozzarella

Fresh mozzarella or buffalo mozzarella often comes with a heavy price tag, but it is a wonderful ingredient that goes a long way, especially if you make the most of all its parts. It is typically sold in a watery brine (also known as whey) that helps keep the cheese fresh and moist. Make sure you keep the cheese in its whey until you are ready to use it, and save the whey to make our Meatballs (p. 185) or to impart your broths and soups with a nice salty, creamy flavor. If you are using fresh mozzarella to top a pizza, let the cheese rest for a few minutes before dressing your pie to allow the excess brine to drain.

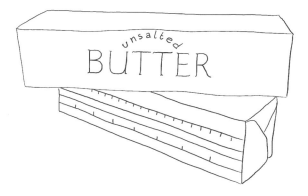

Low-moisture mozzarella

As much as we love fresh mozzarella, there is a time and a place for it, and sometimes a pizza is just begging for some low-moisture mozzarella. (It's the ideal choice for a classic cheese pizza like the Kevin McCallister on p. 101.) Like the name suggests, low-moisture mozzarella (or dry mozzarella) is a type of mozzarella with less moisture that has been salted, aged and slightly dried. It also lends itself better to being grated. Buying pre-grated cheese is tempting (we're busy too, we get it), but by doing so you will end up paying more for a lower-quality product that often comes with a bunch of additives that help prevent the cheese from clumping. We suggest buying a big block of dry mozzarella and grating only what you need when you need it.

Other cheeses

Parmesan (or Parmigiano-Reggiano) is essential for cooking a lot of the recipes in this book and for living a happy life in general. Never buy powdered or pre-grated parmesan—the flavor and texture of those products are usually way off. We always keep a big block in the fridge and love to either shave or Microplane it on pretty much everything, from pastas to salads to roasted vegetables. And in the ethos of making the most with what you've got, make sure to save and freeze your parmesan rinds to make Parmesan Stock (p. 275). We also love to have provolone on hand, whether in block form or sliced (super convenient, especially to top a pizza). Provolone is super versatile and can often be swapped in for dry mozzarella for a bolder-tasting dish.

Butter

You should always have unsalted butter in the fridge. While we love to spread a thick layer of salted cultured butter on a crusty slice of sourdough bread (we're not monsters!), we use unsalted butter for most of our recipes, unless otherwise specified. It's easier to gauge how much salt you add to a recipe that way. Cultured butter goes a long way in adding some oomph to any recipe, except when it comes to baking, since it tends to be less stable.

Eggs

We tested the recipes in this book using large organic eggs. Farm-fresh eggs are best, but if they are not readily available to you, organic or free-range eggs are second and third best. Good-quality eggs will greatly impact the texture and taste of any recipe you're making, but this is even more true when it comes to making fresh egg pasta dough. If you don't believe us, make a batch using regular eggs and another one with fresh farm eggs. The color alone should be enough to convince you.

Cured meats

Most of the meat we use at the restaurant comes from our friends at Aliments Viens and Boucherie Lawrence. Not only does their ethos line up with ours, but they truly have the best meat. For charcuterie like mortadella and salami, we recommend you buy only the amount that you will need for a recipe (and maybe some extra for snacking purposes). Cured meats like pancetta and guanciale have a much longer shelf life, and when tightly wrapped can keep in the freezer for a long time (just take out what you need and store the rest for later use).

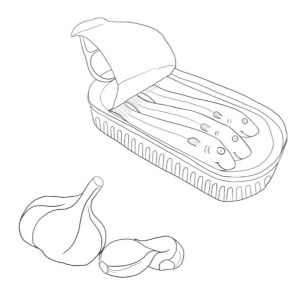

Garlic

We know you know what garlic is, but garlic cloves come in all shapes and sizes. For the sake of clarity and to make sure your recipes don't end up tasting super garlicky, we need to specify that the garlic cloves used to test this book weighed around 5–6 grams (0.2 oz) each. These are the average-size garlic cloves you typically find at the grocery store. If you frequent farmers' markets or have a friend who grows garlic in their backyard, they might have cloves that weigh up to 12 grams (0.4 oz). If that's the case, just halve the amount of garlic in the recipe.

Chilies

We use a lot of different chilies in this book, both fresh and dried. Like with most ingredients, we like to cook with peppers that are grown locally and play around with different levels of heat (we especially love our local variety of Espelette peppers called Gorria). Whenever a recipe calls for dried chili flakes, feel free to use pre-crushed chilies or find whole dried peppers at an Italian grocery store and crush them yourself.

Honey

Instead of grabbing the first bear-shaped squeeze bottle you see on the grocery shelf, do a bit of research to find out who is making great organic honey in your area. Maybe one of your neighbors has a couple of rooftop hives, or perhaps you live somewhere where there are a lot of amazing honey producers. We like to buy our honey from Les Miels d'Anicet, a picturesque farm a few hours north of Montreal run by our friends Anicet Desrochers and Anne-Virginie Schmidt.

Sugar

When it comes to baking, we like to have a few other options on hand besides classic granulated sugar. Organic light brown sugar is a great substitute for granulated sugar in most recipes, and icing sugar can be the perfect finishing touch for cakes, tarts and our Pistachio Cookies (p. 231).

Anchovies

We love anchovies because they can be used to punch up a thousand recipes. Plus, when they're packed in oil or salt, they can keep in the fridge pretty much forever. The price and quality of anchovies can vary greatly. As a rule of thumb, you should always spend more money on anchovies that are going to be one of the shining stars of a dish (like on the Fiore! Fiore! pizza on p. 89) than you would on anchovies that will be blended as part of a sauce (like the Tonnato on p. 264). But if you are anything like our friend Cassady, who's been known to hold us hostage on the phone to argue about anchovies, you should always use the best and most-impossible-to-find silver fish—no matter the recipe.

Aromatics

Here are some basic aromatics you should have before you tackle this book, because we love to use them to infuse our recipes with more flavor: onions, bay leaves, fennel seeds, oregano and coriander seeds. Get a grinder to make sure every spice is super fragrant and fresh. We also like to keep a couple of lemons and oranges rolling around in the fridge drawers—they keep for a long time and can easily be used to spruce up a dish.

EQUIPMENT + TOOLS

Most of the recipes in this book don't require any fancy equipment, but here are some tools that will go a long way toward making your life easier in the kitchen and help you successfully tackle some of our favorite dishes.

Baking sheets
We use baking sheets all the time for almost everything. They're great for toasting nuts, baking cookies, roasting meats, resting dough and drying pasta. They can also be used to cook pizza.

Butcher's twine
We only use this to make the porchetta, but you can also use butcher's twine to tie chicken legs for a perfect roast chicken.

Cast-iron skillet
If you take proper care of your cast-iron skillet, this is the only skillet you will ever need to purchase for the rest of your life. Truly, they last forever. They're great for searing all kinds of meats, frying eggs and more. Just get one and you'll thank us in 50 years.

Cheesecloth
You will be using cheesecloth to make fresh cheeses like ricotta, but in a pinch, you can also use it as a strainer for other things, like when the cork breaks in a bottle of wine and you have to strain it to remove any debris.

Dessert pans and molds
We use a few different sizes of pans and molds for our desserts, including a 12-inch removable-bottom tart pan, 9-inch and 10-inch cake pans, and mini fluted molds. If you don't have the exact size pan the recipe calls for, you can still go ahead and make it, but please note you will have to adjust the baking time accordingly.

Dough scraper
This is an essential tool for any aspiring baker and pasta maker. It makes scraping pieces of dough off the counter so much easier (and you'll avoid getting your fingers all sticky).

Dutch oven or heavy-bottomed saucepan
Dutch ovens with tall sides are ideal for deep-frying, while regular ones will do just fine for simmering and slow-roasting. Heavy-bottomed pans and Dutch ovens are great to ensure your ingredients are cooking evenly.

Food processor, blender and immersion blender
A lot of our sauces benefit from using a food processor or blender to achieve the right texture. You will also need a food processor to make the Semolina Pasta Dough (p. 124).

Food wraps
You will need to use food wraps to keep some doughs from drying out as they rest. Plastic wraps work, but there are also a lot of great brands of reusable beeswax wraps on the market.

Frying thermometer

We haven't included many recipes in this book that involve frying because it can get messy. However, when you do fry, you will want to attach a frying thermometer (also known as a candy thermometer) to the side of your pan to measure the temperature of your oil.

Instant-read thermometer

We love an instant-read thermometer to make sure our meat and fish are cooked perfectly. In this book, we also use it to measure water temperature to make certain cheeses.

Kitchen scale

While we've adapted most of the recipes in this book to use volume measurements (tsp, tbsp and cups) for convenience, we've included weight measurements (grams) for our pizza doughs. Measuring ingredients by weight is much more precise and ensures more consistent results.

Microplane

This is one of the best tools you will ever buy (really, it's something we've even considered bringing on vacation a few times). It's great for zesting citrus, adding a touch of fresh garlic to a dish and finely grating parmesan on salads and pasta.

Pasta roller

There isn't really a substitute for this, so if you are interested in making pasta at home, this is indispensable. Most of the pasta in this book will require you to roll the dough before shaping it.

Piping bag

If you are an avid baker, you are probably very familiar with piping bags. We use them to add filling to stuffed pasta recipes.

Pizza cutter

This is not an essential tool (scissors work too), but we know you had a toy pizza cutter as a kid, and yes, it's just as fun to use the real thing as an adult.

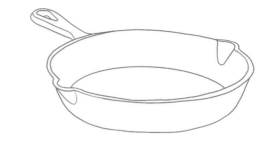

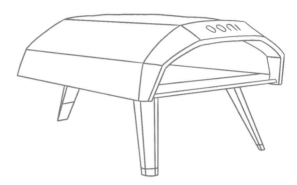

Pizza oven

This is totally optional and there are a lot of pizza oven options out there. We personally like to use Ooni when we are not making pizza at the restaurant.

Pizza peel

If you are serious about making pizza, you should get a pizza peel. It's great to build your pizza on and it makes transferring your pie to the oven a dream. Alternatively, you can use an upside-down baking sheet.

Pizza stone

A pizza stone will help you bake your pizza evenly in a home oven. In a pinch, you can use an upside-down baking sheet instead.

Stand mixer

A stand mixer will make the texture of your doughs more even while saving you lots of time and energy. Technically, all our doughs can be made by hand, but it will take much longer, and results may vary a bit more.

SALADS + VEGETABLES

"The Opposite" is one of our favorite *Seinfeld* episodes of all time. It's the one that begins with a defeated-looking George telling Jerry and Elaine that everything in his life is the opposite of what he wants it to be and that every instinct he has ever had has been wrong. To help George, Jerry convinces him to do the opposite of what he's been doing by saying, "If every instinct you have is wrong, then the opposite would have to be right." This simple decision leads George to turn his life around completely: he orders chicken instead of tuna, gets the girl and lands his dream job with the New York Yankees.

When we were about to open Elena, "The Opposite" sort of became our guiding light. We wanted to turn our lives around, professionally and personally. So we considered our decades of experience working in the service industry and advice from our mentors and ran the other way. It may sound like a terrible idea, but we just knew we couldn't continue working the way we had been.

We had spent the better part of our adult lives curating the perfect dining experiences for others while sacrificing our own well-being. In order to please people and receive external validation in the form of tips or compliments, we would do whatever was needed—from doing shots while holding yoga poses with a guest visiting from out of town to accepting every party invitation thrown at us by regulars. We ended up feeling sad and exhausted. Like George, our lives were the opposite of what we wanted them to be.

For us, choosing to do the opposite wasn't just about breaking the cycle of partying and excess in a world where magnums, shots, butter and foie gras reigned supreme. It quite simply meant we had to learn how to take care of ourselves first so that we could continue to take care of others (think "put your own oxygen mask on before helping others"). We knew how to make other people feel good but had no idea how to do so for ourselves.

Our first baby step in that direction was to put food in our bodies that made us feel alive and vibrant, which is why we wanted the first chapter of our book to be packed with recipes that do just that. This section includes some of our favorite salads and vegetable dishes. There are leafy greens, crunchy-crunch salads and comfortingly rich roasted vegetable platters. There are recipes for fruit heads and recipes for bitter lovers. There are dishes that require hours of preparation and others that come together in only a few minutes. You will also find a few reminders to take it easy and not take yourself too seriously.

Radishes with Pine Nut Puree

SERVES 4–6   SPRING

In Quebec, radishes are a sign that spring is right around the corner and that our long winter is almost over. This fresh, crispy salad is the antidote to the seasonal depression we all inevitably suffer from during that time of year. We like it especially because of the radishes' spicy kick, which jolts us out of hibernation mode and reminds us why it feels so damn good to be alive.

Mix and plate the salad: In a large bowl, combine the quartered radishes, pickled shallots and pickling liquid, lemon juice, salt and pepper. Spread the pine nut puree on a large platter, distribute the dressed radish salad evenly and drizzle with honey. Top with the greens and sprouts, the olive oil and the pan-fried pine nuts. Finish with the crushed chamomile flowers.

Salad

2 lb (900 g) radishes, cut into quarters (about 5 heaping cups)

⅓ cup Pickled Shallots + 2 tbsp pickling liquid (p. 280)

1 tbsp fresh lemon juice

1 tsp flaky sea salt

⅛ tsp freshly ground black pepper

1 batch Pine Nut Puree (p. 261)

2 tbsp wildflower honey

¼ lb (113 g) arugula leaves or nasturtium, trimmed (leaves and flowers are both edible!)

½ cup radish sprouts (optional)

2 tbsp extra virgin olive oil

3 tbsp pan-fried pine nuts (see p. 253)

1 tbsp dried ground chamomile flowers (optional)

Pinzimonio

SERVES 4–6   SPRING + SUMMER

This is our version of a seafood platter—a beautiful vegetable rainbow on a plate—and the culmination of what Elena is all about: deceptively simple but also surprisingly fresh. It's a real showstopper that features the best of what summer has to offer and a great way to feed your friends while you're cooking the rest of the meal. The best pinzimonio requires you to choose your own adventure: Found a bunch of beautiful farm carrots at the market? Scrub them gently and add them to your plate. Got your hands on a purple endive? Flashy watermelon radishes? Add those too! If you want to go the extra mile, double up on dips and serve this with both the pea puree included in the recipe and our Pine Nut Puree (p. 261).

Blanch the peas: Prepare a bowl of ice water. Bring a medium pot of salted water to a boil. Add the peas and blanch until tender but not mushy, 1–2 minutes. Transfer the peas to the ice bath to stop them from cooking any further. Drain the peas. Set aside.

Cook the shallots: In a small frying pan, heat the olive oil over medium heat. Add the shallots, a generous pinch of salt and a few twists of pepper, and cook until the shallots have softened, without browning, 5–8 minutes. Turn off the heat and add 3 tbsp water to stop the cooking. Let it cool down.

Make the puree: In a blender, combine the drained peas, cooled shallot mixture, spinach and mint and process until smooth. Taste and adjust the seasoning with salt and pepper if needed. The pea puree will keep in the fridge for up to 2 days.

Serve: Arrange the raw and pickled vegetables on a large platter in a way that feels fun and beautiful to you. Season with flaky sea salt and serve with the puree.

Special Equipment
Blender

Pea Puree
2 cups shelled fresh peas
6 tbsp extra virgin olive oil
3 medium shallots, thinly sliced
Kosher salt
Freshly ground black pepper
3 tbsp water
2 cups spinach
1 cup fresh mint leaves, lightly packed

Vegetables
1½ lb (680 g) raw vegetables (a mix of cucumber, endive, cherry tomato, sweet pepper, carrot, radish, kohlrabi, turnip and/or fennel), cut into bite-size pieces
½ lb (225 g) pickled vegetables (pp. 279–280 for inspiration)
Flaky sea salt, to finish

Verde

SERVES 4–6   SPRING + SUMMER

Verde Vinaigrette
⅓ cup white wine vinegar
⅓ cup Dijon mustard
¼ cup honey
½ tsp kosher salt
1½ cups vegetable oil
¼ cup extra virgin olive oil

Salad
2 medium or 3 small heads lettuce (like Boston, Batavia or butter; about 8 cups)
3 endives, leaves separated
1 large handful arugula leaves (about 1 cup)
1 small bulb fennel, thinly sliced
¾ cup fresh basil leaves
2 tbsp fresh lemon juice
1 cup grated parmesan
Flaky sea salt
Freshly ground black pepper

We know what you might be thinking: "I don't need a recipe to make a green salad." As much as we hate to be rude, you're wrong on this one. This is the only simple green salad you will ever need to make. Just ask anyone who's ever had it at the restaurant. It's fresh, zippy and punchy and makes you feel like you're doing something great for your soul and your body. The recipe is super simple, but the trick to turn what should be "just another green salad" into "the salad that will change your life" is to choose your greens with care and to eat it with your bare hands (because that's really the only way to eat salad, in our opinion).

Make the vinaigrette: In a medium bowl, whisk the vinegar, Dijon, honey and salt to combine. Slowly add in the vegetable oil to emulsify the vinaigrette. Repeat with the olive oil. The verde vinaigrette will keep in the fridge for up to 1 month.

Mix the salad and serve: In a large bowl, break the lettuce into large pieces. Add the endive leaves, arugula, fennel and basil and mix with your hands. Add vinaigrette to your liking (you will probably end up with some extra, which you can use up throughout the month), lemon juice and parmesan and toss to coat evenly. Taste and adjust the seasoning with salt and pepper. Toss again and serve.

Kale! Caesar!

SERVES 4–6   SPRING + SUMMER

This is the salad equivalent of getting catfished. All the ingredients come together to trick your brain into thinking you're eating a delicious Caesar salad, but there's no mayonnaise and no anchovies anywhere in the recipe. The only thing it has in common with a Caesar are the croutons and the cheese (which we really couldn't live without). Hail, Caesar!

Roast the garlic: Preheat the oven to 350°F. Create a pouch using foil and nestle inside it 10 garlic cloves and 3 tbsp olive oil. Seal up the foil to prevent any oil or steam from escaping. Place the garlic pouch on a baking sheet and roast in the oven until the garlic turns squishy, about 40 minutes. Remove the garlic from the oven but leave the oven on. Open the pouch to let the garlic cool down.

Make the dressing: In a small bowl, whisk together the tahini and cold water until smooth. When the garlic has cooled down a little, add it to a blender along with the tahini mixture, the two remaining raw garlic cloves, vinegar, Dijon and salt. Pulse to combine. With the motor running, gradually add the canola oil (adding it slowly will help emulsify the dressing). Repeat the process with ⅓ cup olive oil. Taste and adjust the seasoning with salt and pepper.

Reheat the garlic croutons: Spread the croutons on a baking sheet and put in the oven to warm up while you make the salad.

Mix the salad: In a large bowl, break the kale into bite-size pieces. Add the radicchio and baby kale and mix with your hands. Add tahini dressing to your liking (you will probably end up with extra dressing, which you can use to make the Chicken Caesar hoagie on p. 219), lemon juice, a generous glug of olive oil, a pinch of salt and a few twists of pepper. Toss to coat evenly. Remove the garlic croutons from the oven and add to the salad along with the grated parmesan. Toss again and serve immediately.

Special Equipment
Blender

Tahini Caesar Dressing (Makes 2 cups)
12 cloves garlic, divided

3 tbsp + ⅓ cup extra virgin olive oil, divided

⅓ cup tahini

2 tbsp cold water

⅓ cup red wine vinegar

¾ tsp Dijon mustard

¾ tsp kosher salt

⅔ cup canola oil

Freshly ground black pepper

Salad
3 cups Garlic Croutons (p. 252)

1 bunch Tuscan kale, stems removed (about 3 cups when cut into bite-size pieces)

1 head radicchio, shredded (about 5 cups)

1 bunch baby kale, stems removed (about 2 cups)

Juice of 1 lemon

Extra virgin olive oil

Flaky sea salt

Freshly ground black pepper

¾ cup finely grated parmesan

Dante Salad

1 head iceberg lettuce, chopped

1 small white onion, thinly sliced and rinsed

25 olives, pitted

1½ cups Pickled Honey Mushrooms (p. 283)

3 tbsp Dante Vinegar (p. 264)

4 tbsp extra virgin olive oil

½ cup shaved provolone

6 oz (170 g) salumi of your choice (we like a mix of Lonza, coppa, salami or ham)

Flaky sea salt and freshly ground black pepper

Dante's was a pizza place in Thornhill, Ontario, where Janice and her family would go all the time. They served this super-heavy pizza with a trashy iceberg lettuce salad that had lots of raw onions, out-of-season tomatoes, cold cuts, pickled hot peppers and sliced cheese, all tossed together in a white vinegar dressing. It was like an Italian sub dumped in a bowl. The whole family was obsessed with it, so much so that years later, Janice decided to create a salad in homage to Dante's, replacing all the trashy ingredients with great ones like homemade pickled honey mushrooms, provolone and nice salumi.

Make the salad: In a large salad bowl, combine the chopped iceberg, sliced onions, olives and pickled honey mushrooms. Dress with Dante vinegar and olive oil, and toss. Top with shaved provolone, salumi and salt and pepper to taste.

Tomatoes and Artichokes with Breadcrumbs

SERVES 4   SUMMER

Janice once described the artichoke as the lobster of the vegetable kingdom, and very few food comparisons have ever sounded so right. Just like lobsters, artichokes are a high-risk, high-reward food. They have a tiny armor with sharp spikes and require a lot of effort to prepare (p. 284). But they're always worth it. If you don't feel like doing all the work to turn and marinate the artichokes yourself (we totally understand!), this recipe will still taste delicious if you use good-quality oil-packed artichokes.

Season the artichokes: Cut the artichokes into halves and quarters (have fun playing around with different sizes and shapes). In a medium bowl, combine the artichokes and the vinegar. Toss and set aside.

Make the salad: Arrange the tomatoes on a platter or in a shallow bowl and season generously with the lemon juice, olive oil, salt and pepper. Top with the artichokes, chives and breadcrumbs.

1½ cups Marinated Artichokes (p. 284) or 6.5 oz (184 g) good-quality jarred artichokes in oil

1½ tbsp red wine vinegar

2 large tomatoes, cut into wedges

Juice of ½ lemon

4 tbsp extra virgin olive oil

Flaky sea salt

Freshly ground black pepper

2 tbsp minced fresh chives

½ cup Toasted Breadcrumbs (p. 251)

Tomato Tonnato

SERVES 4 SUMMER

Fried Capers

½ cup capers, rinsed and drained

¾ cup vegetable oil

Tomato Tonnato Salad

4 large heirloom tomatoes, thinly sliced

Juice of 1 lemon

5 tbsp extra virgin olive oil

Flaky sea salt

Freshly ground black pepper

½ cup Seasoned Breadcrumbs (p. 252)

2 tbsp finely chopped fresh chives

1 cup Tonnato (p. 264)

A few fresh dill flowers or sprigs

When we decided to write this book, our first thought was, "You know what the world needs right now? Another take on vitello tonnato!" Just kidding—nobody needs another version of this classic Piedmontese dish. But because tomato season is so special and because Ryan's and Steph's moms really loved this version, in which savory beefsteak tomatoes play the part of thinly sliced veal, we just had to include it in here.

Fry the capers: Pat and dry the capers. In a frying pan, heat the vegetable oil over medium-high heat. Check to see if the oil is hot enough by adding a single caper—if it sizzles, it's ready to go. Add the capers to the pan and fry until they crisp up and start to look like crystals, about 5 minutes. You'll notice the capers change color and open as they cook. Reduce the heat as necessary to avoid burning. Transfer the capers onto a paper towel–lined baking sheet to absorb the excess oil.

Assemble the salad: Spread the tomatoes evenly onto a large plate. Add the lemon juice, olive oil, salt and pepper. Top with seasoned breadcrumbs, chives and crispy capers. Add a few dollops of tonnato and finish with dill flowers or sprigs.

Grilled Peaches with Pistachios, Peppers and Stracciatella

SERVES 4–6   SUMMER

If you can pick only one dish from this book to cook for your crush, it needs to be this one. Everything about it screams, "I'm ready to go all the way, baby." Jokes aside, this is the peach salad dreams are made of. The spiciness of the peppers, the nutti-ness of the pistachios and the richness of the cheese all come together to complement the sweet juiciness of the peaches. Oh my . . . is it just the grill or is it getting hot in here?

Make the condiment: In a medium bowl, stir to combine the chopped pistachios, pepperoncini in their liquid and simple syrup. Set aside or store in an airtight container in the fridge for up to 1 week.

Cut the peaches: Slice one peach along its natural seam, then gently cup it into your palm to avoid bruising it and twist it to separate the halves. Remove the pit (you can save it to infuse your next batch of simple syrup) and cut the peach into quarters. Repeat with the remaining peaches.

Grill the peaches: Using a pastry brush, coat the peach quarters with 1 tsp olive oil. In a cast-iron skillet (a ribbed cast-iron is even better if you have one), heat 2 tbsp olive oil over medium heat. Gently add the peaches to the skillet and grill each fleshy side until charred, about 30 seconds. Then grill the skin side until shriveled, another 30 seconds. Remove from the heat and cool down slightly. Peel off and discard the skin and cut each peach quarter in half.

Assemble the salad: Distribute the stracciatella on a platter and season with salt. Top with the grilled peaches and drizzle with pistachio condiment. Add a few twists of pepper. Top with Agastache leaves.

Sweet Pistachio Condiment

1 cup toasted pistachios (see p. 253), roughly chopped

2 cups Pepperoncini (p. 286) in their liquid, seeds removed, roughly chopped

⅔ cup Simple Syrup (p. 268)

Peach Salad

4–6 perfectly ripe peaches

1 tsp + 2 tbsp extra virgin olive oil, divided

2 cups Stracciatella (p. 271)

Flaky sea salt

Freshly ground black pepper

1 cup loosely packed fresh Agastache or basil leaves

Cucumbers with Herby Yogurt Dressing and Sesame Seeds

SERVES 4–6   SUMMER

Special Equipment
Blender

Yogurt Dressing
½ cup arugula

½ clove garlic

2 tbsp fresh lemon juice

2 tbsp extra virgin olive oil

½ cup roughly chopped fresh parsley leaves, divided

½ cup picked and roughly chopped fresh dill leaves, divided

½ cup 1-inch-chopped fresh chives, divided

½ cup roughly chopped fresh mint, divided

1 tbsp fresh thyme leaves, divided

1 cup Greek yogurt

Kosher salt and freshly ground black pepper

Cucumber Salad
1½ lb (680 g) cucumbers (preferably a mix of varieties)

1 cup Pickled Shallots (p. 280)

3 tbsp toasted sesame seeds

Flaky sea salt

Freshly ground black pepper

Extra virgin olive oil

Pinch ground Espelette pepper (optional)

A few years ago, Steph got into a bad rock-climbing accident, which forced her to spend a big part of the summer in the hospital. It was a very scary time for all of us, but things could've been a lot worse had she been forced to eat hospital food every day and miss the best of the summer vegetable growing season. Thankfully, we brought her food from Elena almost every day, including this crunchy, tangy and herbaceous cucumber salad. Every bite tastes like summer and friendship, which is especially comforting when you're trapped inside.

Make the yogurt dressing: In a blender, place the arugula, garlic, lemon juice, olive oil and half the herbs (parsley, dill, chives, mint and thyme), saving the rest for garnish. Blend until smooth. Transfer to a bowl and fold in the Greek yogurt. Taste and adjust the seasoning with salt and pepper.

Prepare the cucumbers: Peel the cucumbers if their skins are waxed and remove the seeds if they are large. If not, leave them as is. Cut the cucumbers on an angle into roughly 2-inch pieces, but remember there's no need to be perfect here—just have fun playing around with different shapes.

Assemble the salad: In a bowl, toss the cucumbers with the dressing until each piece is nicely coated. Top with pickled shallots, the remaining chopped herbs and toasted sesame seeds. Season with salt and a few twists of pepper. Finish with a light drizzle of olive oil and a dusting of Espelette pepper.

Zucchini and Roasted Peppers with Salsa Verde

SERVES 4–6   SUMMER

This is like a pasta salad but with vegetables. We love making this recipe with pepper varieties that lie in the middle of the sweet-to-spicy spectrum like Portuguese pepper, Carmen pepper and Corno di Toro. We also like to pick different kinds of zucchinis because the more shapes, sizes and colors, the better this pasta-less pasta salad will taste.

Roast and steam the peppers: Preheat the oven to 450°F and line a baking sheet with parchment paper. Place the peppers on the baking sheet and coat them lightly with olive oil. Bake until the peppers are charred around the edges, turning them halfway, about 20 minutes. Place the peppers inside a covered container to cool and steam for 30 minutes. When the peppers feel cool enough to handle, remove the skins, cores, seeds and stems. Slice them into ½-inch-wide strips.

Prepare the zucchinis: This step can be completed while the peppers are roasting and steaming. Cut both ends of the zucchinis and discard. Use a mandoline or a vegetable peeler to slice the zucchinis into thin strips (think of it as making pappardelle pasta noodles).

Assemble the dish: In a large serving bowl, toss together the zucchini strips, vinegar and salt. Let it rest for a few minutes, after which the zucchinis will look slightly wilted and pliable from the salt and vinegar. Add the roasted pepper strips and salsa verde and toss to combine. Taste and adjust the seasoning if needed. Finish with the shaved ricotta salata and serve.

Special Equipment
Mandoline or vegetable peeler

Zucchini Salad
2 medium red peppers (see above)

1 tsp extra virgin olive oil

5 small zucchinis (about 6 inches long with a 1½-inch diameter)

2 tsp red wine vinegar

1 tsp kosher salt

1 batch Salsa Verde (p. 261)

3½ oz (100 g) ricotta salata, shaved

Ryan's Watermelon Workshop

SERVES 4–6   SUMMER

Dressing

⅓ cup + 2 tbsp dry sherry
(we like La Guita)

⅓ cup Simple Syrup (p. 268)

¼ cup fresh lemon juice

Watermelon Salad

½ cold seedless watermelon,
rind and white removed, cut into
1¼-inch cubes

½ cup roughly torn fresh mint +
a few leaves to garnish

½ cup roughly torn fresh basil
leaves + a few leaves to garnish

⅓ cup Pickled Shallots (p. 280)

Extra virgin olive oil, to drizzle

¼ tsp ground Espelette pepper
or 1 tbsp Chris's Crispy Chili Oil
(p. 256)

½ cup rough shards pecorino

3 tbsp chopped fresh chives or
chive flowers

Ryan takes fruit very seriously. Give him a piece of fruit and he'll tell you a story about it that'll last 45 minutes and end with something like "Oh but wait, you can't get that here." Janice made this watermelon salad one day for a staff meal at the restaurant and Ryan liked it so much that he immediately shouted, "This should be on the menu!" But because it doesn't really feel Italian enough, it never made it. Now it's in this book because we wanted Ryan to have at least one fruit story in his repertoire that ended with "Yes, you can get that."

Make the dressing: In a small bowl, whisk together the sherry, simple syrup and lemon juice. Set aside.

Assemble the dish: In a large bowl, place the watermelon, mint, basil, pickled shallots and dressing. Toss to combine and let it sit for 5 minutes. Drizzle with some olive oil, sprinkle with Espelette pepper and top with pecorino shards and chives. Serve immediately.

Green Beans with Nduja and Almonds

SERVES 4–6 **SUMMER**

We're happy every time we can come up with a recipe that gives us an excuse to eat with our bare hands, and green beans are the perfect finger food (and we're not just saying that because they're shaped like fingers). These beans are fresh, crunchy, smoky and spicy all at the same time—thanks in part to the nduja (a spicy, spreadable Italian pork-based salume). In the summer, wrap the beans in foil and throw them on the grill instead of blanching them, for an extra-smoky version.

Blanch the green beans: Bring a large pot of salted water to a boil. Meanwhile, prepare a large bowl of ice water. Add the green beans to the pot of boiling water and blanch them until just tender, but not soft, about 2 minutes. Using tongs, remove the beans from the water and immediately plunge them in the bowl of ice water until completely chilled. Drain and set aside.

Make the nduja vinaigrette: In a frying pan or a small pot, heat 1 tbsp olive oil over medium-low heat. Add the nduja, sliced shallots and garlic. Using a wooden spoon, break up the nduja to help it render. Continue cooking until the shallots have softened and the nduja is fragrant and rendered, about 7–8 minutes. Remove from the heat, add the sherry vinegar and allow to cool slightly. Add the remaining 1 tbsp olive oil and the water and toss to combine.

Assemble the dish: In a large serving bowl, toss together the green beans, still-warm nduja vinaigrette and toasted almonds. Taste and adjust the seasoning with flaky sea salt. Top with shaved parmesan.

Green Beans

1½ lb (680 g) green beans, trimmed

Nduja Vinaigrette

2 tbsp extra virgin olive oil, divided

3 oz (90 g) nduja, cut into 1-inch cubes (about ¾ cup)

½ shallot, thinly sliced (about 2 tbsp)

1 clove garlic, thinly sliced

2 tbsp sherry vinegar

1 tbsp water

Assembly

1 cup slivered almonds, toasted and coarsely chopped

Flaky sea salt

½ cup shaved parmesan

Fregola Sarda with Fava Beans and Salsa Verde

SERVES 6–8   **SPRING**

2 cups fregola sarda or small pasta of your choice

4 cups fresh or frozen shelled fava beans (about 4 lb/1.8 kg) in the pods)

1 batch Salsa Verde (p. 261)

Kosher salt

Freshly ground black pepper

We like to think of the fregola sarda salad as the Beyoncé of dishes (or Harry Styles or Sting, depending on what generation you're from). Point being that after coming onto the menu as part of a lamb steak dish, the fregola sarda eventually made the ultimate breakaway and went solo, winning the hearts of (roughly) millions.

Cook the fregola sarda: Bring a medium pot of salted water to a boil. Cook the fregola sarda following the directions on the package. Drain, rinse with cold water and transfer to a large mixing bowl. Store in the fridge until ready to use.

Blanch the fava beans: Prepare a bowl of ice water. Bring another pot of salted water to a boil. Add the shelled fava beans and blanch for 1 minute. Transfer the fava beans to the ice bath to stop them from cooking any further. Drain the favas and peel off the outer skins. Set aside.

Mix the salad: In a large bowl, toss to combine the cooked fregola, fava beans and salsa verde. Adjust seasoning with salt and pepper. Let the salad chill in the fridge for an hour before serving to allow the flavors to fully integrate. Serve chilled.

Beans, Beans, Beans

SERVES 4 · ALL SEASONS

In 2019, we were part of this very small group of people (it was mostly our friend Jake Bagshaw) who were trying to make *better beans* a thing. It felt like our movement was starting to pick up steam, but then the pandemic happened and everybody got totally beaned out. We feel like now's the time for beans to make a comeback, and this recipe is the perfect way for them to take the spotlight. If you can find fresh beans at the market in the late summer months (we love borlottis), we suggest buying a big batch, shelling them and storing them in the freezer for later use. Beyond their better taste, using fresh beans also means you get to skip the overnight soaking and get straight to cooking.

Soak the beans: In a large bowl, cover the beans with water by 2 inches (you want to make sure the beans stay covered as they soak and expand). Refrigerate for 12–24 hours, then drain using a colander. If you're in a rush and don't have time to soak the beans overnight, you can do a quick soak by putting the beans in a pot, covering them with water by 2 inches and bringing them up to a boil. Once they're boiling, cover the pot, turn off the heat and let them steep for about 30 minutes. Drain and move on to the next step.

Cook the beans: Preheat the oven to 325°F. Heat a heavy pot with a lid, like a Dutch oven, over medium heat. Add the olive oil and the onions, carrots, celery and garlic. Cook until the vegetables start to sweat, about 2–3 minutes. Add a pinch of salt and throw in the fresh rosemary, thyme, bay leaves, and dried chili flakes. Continue cooking for 3 minutes or so, until the ingredients are fragrant. Pour in the white wine and add the beans and the water, making sure to cover the beans by 1½ inches. Bring the beans to a simmer, then place the lid on the pot and transfer to the oven.

(continued)

Beans

1 cup dried beans of your choice (we love borlotti, baby lima, pinto or Royal Corona beans)

½ cup extra virgin olive oil

½ large onion, peeled, halved from pole to pole

½ carrot, cut into very large chunks

½ stalk celery, cut into very large chunks

½ head garlic, halved across the equator

Pinch + 1 tbsp kosher salt, divided

2 sprigs fresh rosemary

2 sprigs fresh thyme

2 bay leaves

A few pinches dried chili flakes

1 cup white wine

4–5 cups water or low-sodium chicken stock, to cover the beans by 1½ inches while cooking

1–2 tbsp unsalted butter, to reheat (optional)

Juice of ½ lemon, to reheat (optional)

Assembly

4 tbsp Bomba (p. 258) + more to serve

3 tsp extra virgin olive oil

4 tbsp chopped fresh flat-leaf parsley

3 tbsp minced fresh chives

2 tsp fresh lemon juice

Flaky sea salt

Freshly ground black pepper

Sourdough bread

After an hour or so, check to see if the beans are tender but not mushy (depending on the variety and size, the beans can take up to 2 hours to cook). Make sure the beans remain covered with liquid, adding more water or stock if necessary. If the beans need more time, continue cooking and checking for tenderness every 15–20 minutes.

Once tender, remove the beans from the oven and season generously with 1 tbsp salt. Stir and adjust the seasoning to taste. Let cool to room temperature, then pick out (and discard or compost) the vegetables and the aromatics, leaving just the beans in their broth. The beans can be made up to 2 days ahead and kept in their cooking liquid in the fridge. When you're ready to eat, simply reheat the beans with a dab of butter and a squeeze of lemon juice to bring the flavors back to life.

Assemble: Top the beans with the bomba, a generous glug of olive oil, parsley, chives, lemon juice, salt and pepper. Serve with slices of crusty sourdough bread and an extra side of bomba for some added kick.

OUR RULES FOR A PERFECT ROAST

If you know us, you know that we enjoy roasting the people we love. We know that there is a fine line between roasting and burning someone to a crisp, so here are some general guidelines.

1. Get consent. This rule should really apply to everything you do, but it's especially important when it comes to roasting. Upon meeting a new roasting partner, make sure they are OK with being made fun of. If they are not down with it, just drop it. Roasting without the other person being in on the joke is called bullying and that's not cool.

2. Don't take yourself too seriously. Again, this is just amazing advice for life in general, but if you can't make fun of yourself, how in the hell are you going to make fun of someone else? (IYKYK.) Roast yourself whenever possible and let others roast you. We promise, it's a great way to face your insecurities and let go of your ego (and maybe you'll learn to love your early-onset baldness).

3. Be specific. Our favorite type of roast is when someone says something that is so specific it almost feels like they did science paper–level research on us. A truly good roast should make people laugh and make the roastee feel like you're saying, "I noticed all these little things that make you who you are, and I love them. I also want you to know that I see you, so I crafted this joke that now belongs to us forever."

4. Preheat the oven to 425°F and roast, tossing occasionally, until you achieve a nice char on the edges. Be careful not to burn.

Roasted Broccoli with Olive and Almond Pesto

SERVES 4–6   SUMMER

This is the only roast guaranteed to get you praised and not canceled. This recipe makes enough to feed about six people, but we always recommend making a bit more because we've been guilty of eating a whole tray of roasted broccoli before it even makes it onto the plate.

Prepare the broccoli: Preheat the oven to 425°F. Cut each broccoli head into 6–8 large florets. Trim, peel and cut the stems to match the size of the florets.

Roast the broccoli: In a large bowl, toss the broccoli florets and stems with ¼ cup olive oil. Spread the broccoli on a baking sheet in a single layer and roast until it is slightly charred and still has some bite, about 15–20 minutes.

Make the pesto: Meanwhile, place the toasted almonds, olives and garlic cloves in a food processor and pulse until everything is roughly the size of a lentil, about 10 seconds. Transfer to a small bowl and add the shallots, green onions, parsley and ¾ cup olive oil. Toss to combine. You will probably end up with some extra pesto, which will keep in the fridge for up to 1 week and is a great topping for many more roasted vegetables, like cauliflowers, beans and carrots.

Assemble the dish: In a large bowl, toss the warm broccoli with the pesto, the juice of half a lemon, salt and a few twists of pepper. Taste and adjust the seasoning if needed. Transfer to a platter and top with lots of shaved parmesan and a drizzle of olive oil. Serve with a few lemon wedges on the side.

Special Equipment
Food processor

Roasted broccoli
2 large heads broccoli (8 cups florets)
¼ cup extra virgin olive oil

Olive and Almond Pesto
¾ cup toasted almonds (see p. 253)
1 cup green olives, pitted (12 oz/375 ml jar)
2 cloves garlic
1 shallot, finely diced
3 green onions, finely chopped
½ cup chopped fresh parsley leaves
¾ cup extra virgin olive oil

Assembly
2 lemons, divided
Flaky sea salt
Freshly ground black pepper
¼ cup shaved parmesan
Extra virgin olive oil, to drizzle

Roasted Cauliflower with Romesco Sauce

SERVES 4 · AUTUMN

Roasted Cauliflower

2 small heads cauliflower (try to pick different colors), cut into 3-inch florets

3 tbsp extra virgin olive oil

1 tsp kosher salt

Assembly

1 batch Romesco Sauce (p. 267)

Extra virgin olive oil, to drizzle

Fresh lemon juice, to drizzle

Flaky sea salt

¼ cup shaved parmesan

Steph likes to compare this dish to a Big Mac even if it has nothing to do with a burger. We don't all agree, but because she's eaten a lot of Big Macs around the world and has dressed up as a burger for the last seven Halloweens, we will indulge her with this one. Here's her explanation: The cauliflower begins its journey by being roasted and slightly charred before being topped with umami-packed shaved parmesan. According to her, it sort of plays the part of the cheese-topped patty in the Big Mac. Then you have the romesco sauce, which is obviously the Big Mac sauce—it's slightly sweet and tangy, plus it even has a similar color. The dish is finished with a few squeezes of lemon juice, which picks up on the sour-briny flavor that could potentially feel like a pickle if you are truly as deranged as Steph is. But whether you like Big Macs or not, this dish is a formula for satisfaction as a side or a vegetarian main.

Roast the cauliflower: Preheat the oven to 425°F. In a medium bowl, toss the cauliflower florets with the olive oil and salt. Spread the cauliflower onto a baking sheet in a single layer. Roast in the oven until a lot of color has developed and the cauliflower is just becoming tender but still has some bite, 18–25 minutes.

Assemble the dish: Spread the romesco sauce on a large plate or platter. Distribute the roasted cauliflower florets on top, having fun playing with colors and shapes. Dress with extra olive oil and a few squeezes of lemon juice. Finish with salt and shaved parmesan.

Roasted Carrots with Carrot Marmalade and Spicy Honey

SERVES 4 AUTUMN

Roasted carrots are always good and comforting, but they're rarely surprising—this dish is the exception. The carrots are roasted without being blanched first, which means their skins get lightly toasted while the insides turn creamy. We serve them with homemade stracciatella (burrata will work in a pinch), carrot marmalade, spicy honey, a lot of olive oil and hazelnuts. It's the perfect balance of spicy, sweet, salty and fat and a great way to liven up the humble roasted carrot.

Make the carrot marmalade: In a medium pot, heat the butter over medium heat. Cook until it becomes frothy and starts browning, about 4 minutes. Add the grated carrots, honey, water, chili flakes, nutmeg, lemon zest, salt and pepper. Bring to a boil. Reduce the heat to low, cover and gently cook for 30 minutes, checking occasionally that nothing is sticking to the bottom of the pot. Uncover and continue cooking, stirring every so often, until the carrots break down and the texture begins to look like jam, another 30 minutes, for 1 hour total. Taste and adjust the seasoning with salt and pepper.

Roast the carrots: Preheat the oven to 375°F. In a large bowl, toss the carrots with the olive oil, honey, garlic, thyme and a generous amount of salt and pepper. Spread on a baking sheet and roast, tossing occasionally, until the skins begin to pucker and caramelize, 45 minutes to 1 hour. The carrots should become slightly tender but still retain a bit of bite.

Assemble the dish: Dollop warm carrot marmalade on a serving platter and pile on the roasted carrots. Squeeze the garlic cloves out of their peels over the carrots. Break the stracciatella into small strands with your hands and distribute evenly. Drizzle on spicy honey and olive oil, and season with flaky sea salt and freshly ground black pepper. Garnish with crushed hazelnuts and greens and serve warm.

Carrot Marmalade

4 tbsp unsalted butter

4 large carrots, peeled and grated (about 3½ cups)

¼ cup wild honey

1 cup water

½ tsp dried chili flakes

¼ tsp freshly grated nutmeg

Finely grated zest of ½ lemon

½ tsp kosher salt

½ tsp freshly ground black pepper

Roasted Carrots

2 lb (900 g) small farm carrots, scrubbed

1 tbsp extra virgin olive oil

2 tbsp honey

1 head garlic, cut in half

5 sprigs fresh thyme

Kosher salt

Freshly ground black pepper

Assembly

1 cup Stracciatella (p. 271), room temperature

4–5 tsp Spicy Honey (p. 257)

Extra virgin olive oil

Flaky sea salt

Freshly ground black pepper

¾ cup roasted hazelnuts (see p. 253), roughly chopped

1 cup spicy mustard greens or arugula (optional)

Cicoria alla Romana with Bottarga

SERVES 4 **AUTUMN**

Greens

⅓ cup extra virgin olive oil

½ tsp dried chili flakes

5 anchovy fillets

2 lb (900 g) bitter greens of your choice, chopped into 4-inch pieces

2 tsp minced garlic

Kosher salt

Juice of 1 lemon

Assembly

½ lobe bottarga (cured fish roe)

Life's all about making the most with what you've got. So, when things get bitter (like these winter greens), just drown everything in olive oil, add some salt and take your time with it. We promise it gets better—delicious even. For this recipe, we suggest adding a bit of color to your day with a combination of hearty greens like radicchio, endive, Treviso, sugarloaf or dandelion. These greens are also great the next day served with eggs on toast.

Cook the greens: In a large pan, heat the olive oil, dried chili flakes and anchovies over medium-high heat. Cook until you notice the anchovies start to "melt" into the oil, lowering the heat as necessary to prevent burning. Add the greens and toss them in the hot oil until they begin to wilt slightly, 1–2 minutes. Add the garlic and a couple pinches of salt, and continue cooking until the greens are pleasantly tender, about 4 minutes. Remove from the heat and add the lemon juice. Taste and adjust the seasoning.

Assemble the dish: Spread on a platter or large plate and finish by grating the bottarga over the top using a Microplane.

Radicchio and Citrus Salad with Black Olives

SERVES 4–6   WINTER

We really wanted to make something with radicchio for our friend Myrtha Zierock, who helped spread radicchio awareness across the province when she lived in Montreal. Now that she's back home in the Dolomites working alongside her mother, legendary winemaker Elisabetta Foradori, and growing the most beautiful radicchios and chicory plants we've ever seen, we wanted to honor her with a salad that's as sunny and bright as she is.

Make the orange vinaigrette: In a small bowl, whisk together the confit orange puree, wine vinegar and olive oil to emulsify. Set aside.

Prepare the citrus: Segment and chop your fruits into cubes if you're using larger varieties like grapefruits and pomelos. For smaller citrus like oranges and tangerines, use a paring knife to remove the peel and pith, then slice each fruit into ⅛-inch-thick wheels.

Assemble the salad: In a large bowl, vigorously toss the torn radicchio with the orange vinaigrette, salt and pepper. Add the olives, shallots and prepared citrus and toss gently to combine. Taste and adjust the seasoning with salt and pepper. Top with sunflower sprouts and serve immediately.

Orange Vinaigrette
⅓ cup Confit Orange Puree (p. 269)

2 tbsp wine vinegar of your choice

½ cup extra virgin olive oil

Salad
4–6 citrus fruits (preferably a mix of pomelo, blood orange, tangerine, Minneola or grapefruit)

2 heads radicchio, torn (roughly 8 cups)

Flaky sea salt

Freshly ground black pepper

½ cup black olives (preferably a drier variety like Moroccan), pitted and torn in half

1 shallot, thinly sliced in rings

½ cup sunflower sprouts or arugula

PIZZA

Why pizza? It's simple. Everybody loves pizza. It's what every kid wants to eat on their birthday. It's what you order when your friends help you move. It's what you eat after a fun night out. Pizza brings people together. And that's exactly what we want to do at Elena.

When we signed the lease for a nondescript building that used to house a strip club deep in St-Henri, we had no idea what we were doing. We had no money or investors. All we knew is that we wanted to do what nobody else was doing and make the best naturally leavened pizza in Montreal (a style of pizza dough made with sourdough starter instead of commercial yeast) using locally sourced ingredients. We think we did a pretty good job, but we would've never been able to do it alone.

A lot of our early successes can be attributed to our friend Jake "Bigsby" Bagshaw. Armed with a true passion for all things dough (his family runs Bigsby the Bakehouse in Vancouver), Jake came on board at the very beginning to help us develop our first naturally leavened pizza dough. It was a grueling process that took several months (we ate so much pizza!), but Jake never wavered. We opened the restaurant with pizza we were proud of and Jake continued to improve it until his last day with us.

Then Chris Cameron came along. With years of experience as a pizzaiolo under his belt, he brought our pizza program to the next level and launched a hoagie revolution. For this book, we wanted to develop recipes that could be made in a home kitchen while remaining as close as possible to what we do at the restaurant. Chris helped us make that wish a reality.

This is by no means a technical pizza book. (There are plenty of other books out there if you want to deepen your skills.) Think of *Salad Pizza Wine* as the beginning of your pizza journey.

In the next pages, we will show you how to make, proof and stretch Neapolitan and al taglio pizza doughs using natural or store-bought yeast. We tested each of these dough recipes in Montreal, a city with extreme weather conditions (winters so cold that the air hurts your face, and summers so hot and sticky that Marley can barely stand wearing anything but tiny tank tops and even tinier shorts). Because pizza dough is a living organism (you will notice how much it moves once you make it for the first time), it is greatly impacted by its environment. This means you probably will have to adapt our dough recipe to your unique surroundings. If you don't know what any of this means just yet, don't worry, these recipes will work just about anywhere. But the more pizza you make through the seasons, the more you will notice the small shifts in your dough and learn to tweak it.

At the restaurant, we bake our pizzas in a custom-built wood-fire oven that reaches temperatures over 900°F. While it makes incredible pizza with a stunning leopard-patterned crust, we know that kind of equipment is not accessible to everyone (it was complicated enough for us to build one). We tested all the pizza recipes in this book in a home oven at 500°F. Although the final result will never taste exactly the way it does at the restaurant, we provide you with enough tips to bring your pies as close to the real thing as possible. (If you are lucky enough to own a gas-powered pizza oven like the ones made by Ooni, you will be able to achieve results closer to what we make at Elena.)

The first part of this chapter is dedicated to Neapolitan pizza, the round pie with a super-airy crust most people know us for. The last part of the chapter features four al taglio recipes, a thicker, rectangular Roman style of pizza that's often baked in a normal oven. By now, you know how much we love the idea of choosing your own adventure in the kitchen, and making pizza is no exception. That's why we made sure you can use all our Neapolitan pie recipes to make al taglios (just quadruple the amount of sauce and toppings).

Whatever pizza you end up making first, make sure to loosen up. Pizza should be fun! What if you mess up? Just start over and make a double batch of dough in case it happens again. Like most things in life, the more you do it, the more confident you'll get at it. Embrace the learning curve. Plus, no one will ever be mad at you for making too much pizza while you're still getting your bearings. Remember: everybody loves pizza.

Sourdough Starter

MAKES A POTENTIALLY NEVER-ENDING SUPPLY TO SHARE WITH YOUR FRIENDS

Making and keeping a sourdough starter can be a pain at first, but it will bring the taste of your pizza dough and bread to the next level. If none of your friends have a sourdough starter at home, making your own is easy if you follow these simple steps.

All-purpose flour

Warm water

Whole wheat flour, rye flour or flour of your choice (to feed your starter)

Day 1: In a container with a lid (a mason jar or a plastic container work fine), combine ¼ cup all-purpose flour with ½ cup very warm water (86°F–95°F) and mix, making sure to leave a few inches at the top for the starter to expand. Place the container somewhere warm (a turned-off oven with the light on works well).

Day 2: After 24 hours, the mixture should be bubbling and sour, meaning the fermentation process has started. If it hasn't, wait another 12 hours and check again. Add ¼ cup all-purpose flour and mix to combine. Return the jar to its cozy spot.

Day 3: The starter should now be bubbling more and have gained in volume due to fermentation. Discard all but roughly 2 tbsp of the starter mixture and add ¼ cup flour of your choice and ¼ cup warm water (about 75°F–82°F). This is your daily starter feed.

Happily ever after: The fermentation should be stable after day 3 and your starter should now smell like yogurt and have peaked in volume. To test it, flick 1 tsp starter in a bowl of warm water. If it floats, it's ready. You can now feed your starter daily with wheat or rye flour, discarding all but roughly 2 tbsp of starter mix and adding your starter feed (¼ cup flour of your choice and ¼ cup warm water). After several feedings, you'll start to notice your starter rise and fall throughout the day—this is normal.

If you're baking regularly, your starter should be fed daily, stored in a sealed container and kept between 68°F and 86°F. If you're not baking regularly, your starter can be stored in the fridge without feeding for up to 30 days. When you're ready to use it again, take it out of the fridge and repeat each step starting from day 3. It should be ready to use the next day. Keep in mind that the more mature a starter is, the more sourness will be exhibited in the final product. A healthy starter will keep for years.

Naturally Leavened Neapolitan Pizza Dough

MAKES 4 NEAPOLITAN DOUGH BALLS

You know what they say: once you go naturally leavened, you never go back. At the risk of repeating ourselves, we just can't stress enough how big a difference natural yeast makes when it comes to the taste and texture of pizza dough. If you're lucky, you might also end up like Marley, who against all odds, got super ripped after he started eating naturally leavened pizza every single day. This recipe yields four dough balls, but if this is your first time making pizza, we suggest doubling it. The extra dough will come in handy if you encounter any issues during the stretching and baking process. Plus, any leftover dough will keep tightly wrapped in the freezer for months.

Hydrate the flours: Bakers refer to this step as autolyze—it basically allows the flour and water to create a loose structure before we incorporate the sourdough starter. If using a stand mixer: In the bowl of the stand mixer fitted with a hook attachment, add the water first [1], followed by the flours [2]. Mix on low until fully combined, about 4 minutes at the lowest speed [3]. Turn the mixer off and let the dough rest in the bowl for 20 minutes. If mixing by hand: In a large bowl, add the water first [5], followed by the flours [6]. Mix until fully combined, about 8 minutes—use a rubber spatula at first and then your hands once the dough starts coming together [7]. Let the dough rest in the bowl for 20 minutes.

Mix or knead the dough: Add the sourdough starter and salt and continue to mix on the same speed or knead the dough until it is supple and homogeneous, about 9–12 minutes [4, 8].

Fold the dough and let it rise: Lightly oil the inside of a large airtight container. Transfer the dough to the container and, beginning with the edge farthest away from you, grab the dough from underneath and fold it up and toward you. (This motion should be done confidently to stretch the dough without ever tearing it.) Now, rotate the container 90 degrees and repeat the same process until the dough has been folded on itself for a total of four times. Cover the dough and rest it at room temperature for 30 minutes. Repeat the folding process two more times, resting the dough 30 minutes at the end of each folding session.

Special Equipment

Mixer (optional)

Large 4-inch-deep airtight container

Four ½-pint containers with lids (optional)

Dough scraper

1½ cups (375 ml) water (65°F)

3 cups (453 g) all-purpose flour

½ cup + 2 tsp (80 g) whole wheat flour

½ cup + 1 tbsp (107 g) Sourdough Starter (p. 67)

1 scant tbsp (13 g) fine sea salt

Extra virgin olive oil, to oil the container

Semolina rimacinata or all-purpose flour, to dust your work surface

(continued)

Divide the dough: Transfer the dough to a lightly floured surface and, using a dough scraper, divide it into four even pieces. Lightly oil and flour the inside of the same container if you have enough space for it in your fridge. Alternatively, you can use four smaller containers, one for each dough ball. Using separate containers will allow you to work with only one dough ball at a time, which will make it easier when it comes time to cook your pizzas.

Shape the dough into balls: Watch out for this next step—a surface with too much or too little flour can make shaping the balls difficult. You want to put just enough flour for there to be some stickiness to help shape the ball, but not so much that the ball will just slip around the table. If you notice the dough is sticking to your hands too much as you are shaping the ball, bury your hands in flour for a moment instead of adding more to the dough or the work surface. Working with one dough portion at a time, fold each corner toward the center of the ball [1, 2]. Place the dough seam side down on the table and, applying moderate pressure, gently press your hand on the dough, moving it in a circular motion until you have a smooth ball [3, 4]. A well-shaped ball should be evenly round and taut, with no tears or large air bubbles. Overworking the dough during this step can cause it to tear [5], but don't worry if this happens—simply set it aside and let it rest for a few minutes while you work on the next ball. After a few minutes, you will be able to repeat the process and form a nice smooth ball [6]. Place each shaped ball, seam side down, on an oiled and floured baking sheet or in a container. Cover or seal and chill in the fridge for 2 days.

Yeasted Neapolitan Pizza Dough

1½ cups (375 ml) water (65°F)

4 cups (600 g) all-purpose flour

3 tbsp + 1 tsp (30 g) whole wheat flour

1 tbsp (15 g) fine sea salt

1⅛ tsp (4 g) instant dry yeast

Extra virgin olive oil

Semolina rimacinata or all-purpose flour, to dust your work surface

No starter? No problem. This is the yeasted version of our Neapolitan dough. It doesn't pack the same oomph as the naturally leavened version, but it's easy to make and needs to ferment in the fridge for only 24 hours instead of two days.

Follow the steps on page 69: When it is time to mix or knead the dough, add the salt and yeast (instead of the sourdough starter) and continue to mix on the same speed or knead the dough until it is supple and homogeneous, about 9–12 minutes. Continue to follow the steps on page 69; when the dough balls have been placed in the lightly oiled container, cover and chill in the fridge for 24 hours (instead of 2 days).

Stretching and Baking

Special Equipment
Pizza stone (optional)
Pizza peel (optional)

There are many different techniques for stretching out pizza dough, and many of them take months or even years to master. Some cooks use a slapping technique, while others do a steering-wheel movement, gradually working their way around the dough. Others do like in the movies, tossing the dough in the air and catching it at the precise moment it has reached the perfect size. The easiest and most straightforward method, which is what we teach you here, is to stretch the dough out on a flat surface until you achieve a 10-inch circle.

These directions call for a pizza stone and a pizza peel, but you can still make great pizza without any fancy tools. We did some tests where we cooked a few pizzas on an inverted baking sheet, and they turned out delicious. Making good pizza is not about being flashy. So you might want to start with what you already have until you're ready to splurge on pizza equipment.

When baking your pizza, keep in mind that every home oven is a bit different. Perhaps yours has a hot spot in the back, which means you might have to rotate your pizza halfway through to get it evenly charred. Maybe your oven runs hotter than 500°F, which means you could crank up the heat and cook your pizza for a shorter amount of time. Follow our directions for your first pie and then feel free to adapt them according to your liking and the equipment you have at your disposal. You got this.

Position the rack and preheat the oven: Place a rack in the lower third of the oven and remove the rack above it. Slide the pizza stone on the rack and turn up your oven to 500°F. Let the stone preheat for at least 1 hour before baking your pizza. (If you don't have a pizza stone, you can bake the pizza directly on an inverted baking sheet without preheating it.)

Temper the dough: Make sure you time this step according to the amount of preparation required for your toppings and the preheating of your pizza stone. Depending on the pie you are making, you might want to start tempering your dough while you are prepping your toppings or only after you've laid out everything. Warm dough will stretch faster but will be more prone to holes, while dough that is too cold will require more time and strength to stretch out. Once your dough has had enough time to ferment and you are ready to make your pizza, remove it from the fridge and temper for a minimum of 20 minutes on the counter [1].

Set up your pizza station: Make sure you have all your toppings and tools at the ready, because once your dough is stretched, you'll want to start building your pizza right away. We're talking sauces, cheeses, meats, herbs, flours, pizza peel, ladle, cooling rack and pizza cutter.

Check your dough: Gently press a finger into the dough to see if it's ready. It should feel supple to the touch and come back slowly

(continued)

after being poked. If it feels too stiff, leave it out for a few minutes, checking often to make sure it doesn't overproof.

Stretch the dough: Working one dough ball at a time, carefully cut the edges of the ball to separate it from the others, and transfer to a well-floured surface like a countertop. If you stored your dough in individual containers, skip this step and, instead, gently flip the container over a small mound of flour. Be mindful of how you handle the dough—you want to preserve its round shape and avoid creating holes as you move it. It is also important to keep the top and the bottom facing the same way throughout. Make sure both the top and the bottom are well floured before you begin stretching out the dough.

Using your fingertips, begin by pressing a rough round shape in the center of the dough ball, allowing for a 1½-inch border [2, 3], which will become your crust (you want to keep the air in the crust, so avoid pressing the dough around the edges throughout the process). Once you have established the inner ring, gently press down the dough inside the ring, gradually stretching it out in a circular motion [4, 5]. Add more flour underneath the dough if needed. If your dough still needs more stretching, carefully slide your hands underneath it to open it up some more [6, 7]. With practice, you can start moving your hands in a circular motion to stretch your dough. Continue until you have stretched your dough to about 10 inches.

(continued)

Transfer the dough onto the peel: Flour your pizza peel, then shake it gently to remove any excess flour. There should be enough flour on the peel so that your pizza can move around freely without sticking, but not so much that it bakes into the bottom of the crust, making it mealy and floury. Using your hands, gently transfer the stretched dough onto the pizza peel, making sure it retains its round shape [8, 9].

Build the pizza: Once the sauce and cheese go on, there is no turning back, so make sure your oven and stone are nice and hot. Sauce and top your pizza following the recipe, always making sure to leave 1½ inches of uncovered dough around the edges for the crust [10, 11, 12]. Remember to apply only light pressure to avoid poking holes in the dough as you are doing this.

Bake the pizza: Take the peel (or other transfer tool) and insert it into the oven at a slight angle until you reach the back of the pizza stone. Give the peel a little shake to allow the pizza to start sliding off it—it should look like you are draping the pizza from the back of the stone to the front.

Bake the pizza for 8–10 minutes, until the center has set and the crust has formed nice golden and blistered bubbles. Note that every home oven heats a little differently. You may want to experiment with switching to a broil setting for the last couple of minutes of cooking to mimic the doming effect of a wood-fire oven and achieve a leopard-like charred pattern. The more you use your oven to make pizza at home, the more you'll be able to nail the perfect cooking time and technique. (If you don't have a pizza stone, you can bake your pizza directly on an inverted baking sheet for the first 8 minutes, then finish cooking it directly on the rack until the dough is nice and crisp.)

Rest the pizza: Once you are satisfied with the bake of your pizza, use the peel to remove it from the oven (or use tongs to grab the edge of the pizza) and transfer it onto a cooling rack. Let it rest for 1 minute.

Finish the pizza and serve: Transfer the pizza to a cutting board or a pizza pan. Add any finishing touches, cut into six slices and serve.

FUCK, MARRY, KILL

People usually play this game using celebrity names but we like to play with food because people's answers can reveal so much about their personality. Imagine thinking someone's your friend only to find out they'd rather marry mayonnaise over olive oil (don't even get us started on people who kill butter). Here are some of our favorite combinations but feel free to make up your own. Remember, there are no right or wrong answers (except when there are).

CITRUS, STONE FRUITS, BERRIES

MORTADELLA, PEPPERONI, LARDO

PIZZA, PASTA, HOAGIE

BUTTER, OLIVE OIL, MAYONNAISE

PORK, CHICKEN, BEEF

PARMESAN, RICOTTA, MOZZARELLA

ALMOND, PISTACHIO, PINE NUT

Margherita

We all know that the margherita is the benchmark when it comes to pizza. What you may not know about us is that when we first opened the restaurant, we were so clueless about what we were doing (and clearly overwhelmed) that when our friend Kyle ordered a margherita, we brought him a margarita cocktail instead. It wasn't even on the menu. It's embarrassing to admit, but thankfully we've gotten a lot better at taking orders and making pizza since that first night. This is a great margherita.

1 ball Neapolitan Pizza Dough (p. 69 or 70)

¼ cup canned crushed tomatoes

1 ball (2½ oz/75 g or about ½ cup) buffalo mozzarella

1 tbsp extra virgin olive oil + more to finish

6–8 leaves fresh basil

Before you can start building your pizza: Follow the instructions in the Stretching and Baking section (p. 73) to position the rack and preheat the oven, temper the dough, set up your pizza station, stretch the dough, and transfer it onto the pizza peel. Once those steps are complete, you're ready to build your pizza.

Sauce the pizza: Dollop the crushed tomatoes in the center of the pizza and, with the back of a spoon, gently spread the sauce in a circular outward motion, leaving 1½ inches of uncovered dough around the edges for the crust. Be careful not to apply too much pressure to avoid damaging the dough.

Top the pizza: Break up the mozzarella with your hands and spread it evenly over the sauce. Drizzle the pizza with 1 tbsp olive oil.

Bake and rest the pizza: Follow the directions in the Stretching and Baking section (p. 73).

Finish the pizza and serve: Drizzle the pizza with more olive oil, transfer to a cutting board or pizza pan, cut and top with a few fresh basil leaves.

Dany

MAKES 1 (10-INCH) PIZZA   SPRING + AUTUMN

1 ball Neapolitan Pizza Dough
(p. 69 or 70)

1 clove garlic, finely minced

2 tbsp extra virgin olive oil

1 large handful big-leaf spinach
(about 1 cup packed)

Kosher salt

Freshly ground black pepper

1 ball (2½ oz/75 g or about
½ cup) buffalo mozzarella

⅓ cup grated low-moisture
mozzarella

1 tsp sesame seeds

1 tsp Spicy Honey (p. 257)

If you grew up or partied in Montreal anytime between 1998 and 2014, there's a good chance you ended up eating a slice at Pizza Dany on de la Montagne. It was also the place we used to go to after we finished working long nights at Nora Gray. Steph and our friend Nick Rosati (who now co-owns Crèmerie Dalla Rose and Cafè A Posto) would go there all the time on their way back to the Plateau and would joke about getting pulled over for "overeating and driving" as they wolfed down greasy slices of spinach pizza with sesame seeds. Being able to make our version of Dany's famous spinach pizza is our way to still indulge and reminisce about those years now that our partying days are behind us.

Before you can start building your pizza: Follow the instructions in the Stretching and Baking section (p. 73) to position the rack and preheat the oven, temper the dough, set up your pizza station, stretch the dough, and transfer it onto the pizza peel. Once those steps are complete, you're ready to build your pizza.

Prepare the toppings: In a medium bowl, whisk together the minced garlic and olive oil. Add the spinach, salt and pepper and toss until the spinach leaves are well coated in garlic oil. Set aside.

Top the pizza: Break the buffalo mozzarella into small pieces with your fingers and disperse it evenly over the pizza, leaving 1½ inches of uncovered dough around the edges for the crust. Add the low-moisture mozzarella in a similar fashion. Place the dressed spinach over the cheese in one even layer and sprinkle the whole pie with sesame seeds.

Bake and rest the pizza: Follow the directions in the Stretching and Baking section (p. 73).

Finish the pizza and serve: Drizzle the cut pizza with spicy honey, close your eyes and imagine it's 4 a.m. Enjoy!

Giardino

MAKES 1 (10-INCH) PIZZA   SPRING + SUMMER

Every year, we set up a garden behind the restaurant where we grow a bunch of herbs and flowers that we use as garnish on some of our dishes. The pizza giardino is an off-menu item that exists only when everything in the garden is in full bloom and when someone on staff has an extra 20 minutes to pick fresh herbs out back. All that to say, this pizza is a rare occurrence and it's probably easier for you to make at home than for us to make it for you. Be careful: because this pizza highlights freshly picked herbs, you bake the dough prior to adding any toppings.

Before you can start building your pizza: Follow the instructions in the Stretching and Baking section (p. 73) to position the rack and preheat the oven, temper the dough, set up your pizza station, stretch the dough, and transfer it onto the pizza peel.

Poke the dough: Using a fork, poke a few holes in the dough, avoiding the crust.

Bake and rest the pizza: Follow the directions in the Stretching and Baking section (p. 73).

Prepare the toppings: While the pizza is baking, toss the picked herbs and greens lightly in olive oil. Add the pickled shallots and almonds, and toss. Season with salt and pepper to taste. Set aside.

Top the pizza and serve: Spread the pistachio pesto on the baked dough, avoiding the crust. If using buffalo mozzarella, break it into small pieces with your hands before spreading it evenly over the pizza. Cut the pizza and top with the dressed greens, shallots and almonds. Enjoy immediately before the leaves start to wilt.

1 ball Neapolitan Pizza Dough (p. 69 or 70)

1½ cups freshly picked herbs and greens (we like a mix of arugula, sage, mint, basil, chives or dill), torn if large

1 tsp extra virgin olive oil

1½ tbsp Pickled Shallots (p. 280), drained

1½ tbsp toasted slivered almonds or sesame seeds

Flaky sea salt

Freshly ground black pepper

¼ cup Pistachio Pesto (p. 265)

1 ball (2½ oz/75 g or about ½ cup) buffalo mozzarella or ½ cup Stracciatella (p. 271)

Marinara Bianca

MAKES 1 (10-INCH) PIZZA   SUMMER

2 heirloom tomatoes

1½ tsp kosher salt

1 tbsp minced green onions

1 tsp capers, rinsed

1 tsp extra virgin olive oil + more to finish

1 ball Neapolitan Pizza Dough (p. 69 or 70)

1 tsp fresh oregano leaves, picked

Fresh mustard greens

Flaky sea salt

Freshly ground black pepper

We love making this pizza using capers grown by winemaker Gabrio Bini in Pantelleria, Italy. But just like his wines, his capers are quite hard to find and expensive. Since the success of this recipe hinges on the quality of the ingredients, we still recommend taking the time to find good-quality capers. And if you need help, we know a guy.

Prepare the tomatoes: Bring a medium pot of salted water to a boil and prepare a bowl of ice water. Remove the core of the tomatoes and score with an x at the bottom. Carefully plunge the tomatoes into the boiling water until the skins start to loosen slightly, about 30 seconds. Transfer the tomatoes to the ice bath for about 1 minute. Remove the skins, then cut the tomatoes along the equator. Salt the cut sides of the tomato halves and place cut side down in a colander set over a bowl. Let the tomatoes drain for 2 hours at room temperature or overnight in the fridge, until they have lost about 20 percent of their water weight. Tear the drained tomatoes into bite-size pieces and put in a small bowl, along with the green onions, capers and olive oil. Toss to combine and set aside.

Before you can start building your pizza: Follow the instructions in the Stretching and Baking section (p. 73) to position the rack and preheat the oven, temper the dough, set up your pizza station, stretch the dough, and transfer it onto the pizza peel. Once those steps are complete, you're ready to build your pizza.

Sauce the pizza: Dollop the tomato mixture in the center of the pizza and, with the back of a spoon, gently spread it in a circular outward motion, leaving 1½ inches of uncovered dough around the edges for the crust.

Bake and rest the pizza: Follow the directions in the Stretching and Baking section (p. 73).

Top the pizza and serve: Dress the baked pizza with fresh oregano and mustard greens. Finish with olive oil, flaky sea salt and freshly ground black pepper.

Diavolo 2.0

MAKES 1 (10-INCH) PIZZA   ALL SEASON

The Diavolo 1.0 was topped with pepperoni we made in house because we were ambitious and committed to doing everything ourselves (this is a nice way to say we were foolish). Eventually we figured out that in pizza, like in life, you must choose your battles, and charcuterie wasn't going to be one of them for us. That's why we started buying our pepperoni from our friend Phil Viens and changed the name of the pizza to Diavolo 2.0 because it truly felt like an upgrade on what we were doing before. We still make the pepperoncini ourselves though, and so should you (p. 286).

1 ball Neapolitan Pizza Dough (p. 69 or 70)

¼ cup crushed tomatoes

1 ball (2½ oz/75 g or about ½ cup) buffalo mozzarella

¼ cup grated auricchio (spicy provolone)

2 oz (60 g) thinly sliced salami

2 tbsp Pepperoncini (p. 286)

Before you can start building your pizza: Follow the instructions in the Stretching and Baking section (p. 73) to position the rack and preheat the oven, temper the dough, set up your pizza station, stretch the dough, and transfer it onto the pizza peel. Once those steps are complete, you're ready to build your pizza.

Sauce the pizza: Dollop the crushed tomatoes in the center of the pizza and, with the back of a spoon, gently spread the sauce in a circular outward motion, leaving 1½ inches of uncovered dough around the edges for the crust. Be careful not to apply too much pressure to avoid damaging the dough.

Top the pizza: Break the buffalo mozzarella into chunks with your fingers and spread it all over the sauce. Sprinkle the grated auricchio over the top, avoiding the crust area, then evenly disperse the salami slices on top.

Bake and rest the pizza: Follow the directions in the Stretching and Baking section (p. 73).

Finish the pizza and serve: Finish the pizza by adding the pepperoncini.

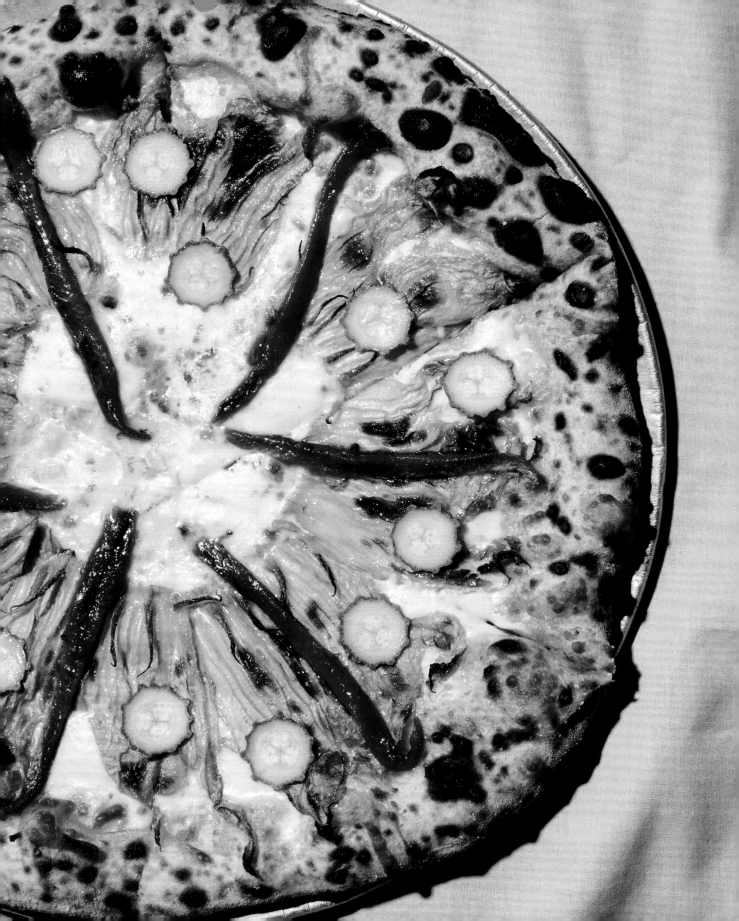

Fiore! Fiore!

MAKES 1 (10-INCH) PIZZA   SUMMER

Inspired by Gabriele Bonci's zucchini flower pizza at Bonci in Rome, this is a good vibes–only pizza that embodies the peak of summer joy when zucchini blossoms are in season. Plus, if you close your eyes, the tiniest bite of this pizza will transport you straight to the city of Romulus and Remus.

Before you can start building your pizza: Follow the instructions in the Stretching and Baking section (p. 73) to position the rack and preheat the oven, temper the dough, set up your pizza station, stretch the dough, and transfer it onto the pizza peel. Once those steps are complete, you're ready to build your pizza.

Top the pizza: Spread the garlic slices evenly on the surface of the pizza. Break the buffalo mozzarella into chunks and scatter evenly, leaving 1½ inches of uncovered dough around the edges for the crust. Sprinkle the low-moisture mozzarella over the top, avoiding the crust. Place the zucchini flowers in a sunburst with their petals facing the outside. Drizzle with 1 tsp olive oil and season lightly with salt and pepper.

Bake and rest the pizza: Follow the directions in the Stretching and Baking section (p. 73).

Finish the pizza and serve: In a small bowl, toss the zucchini slices with the stamens in their liquid, 1 tsp of salt and a pinch of pepper. Disperse evenly over the baked pizza. Cut it into six slices, then top each slice with one anchovy fillet.

1 ball Neapolitan Pizza Dough (p. 69 or 70)

1 clove garlic, thinly sliced

1 ball (2½ oz/75 g or about ½ cup) buffalo mozzarella

⅓ cup grated low-moisture mozzarella

6 zucchini flowers, opened with stamen and base removed

2 tsp extra virgin olive oil, divided

Kosher salt

Freshly ground black pepper

¼ cup thinly sliced zucchini coins

6 pickled zucchini stamens + 2 tbsp Basic Pickling Brine (p. 279; optional)

6 anchovy fillets

Mortadella, Artichokes, Pistachio

MAKES 1 (10-INCH) PIZZA SUMMER

1 ball Neapolitan Pizza Dough
(p. 69 or 70)

1 ball (2½ oz/75 g or about
½ cup) buffalo mozzarella

⅓ cup grated low-moisture
mozzarella

5 Marinated Artichokes
(p. 284), roughly torn

6 slices mortadella

2 tbsp Pistachio Pesto (p. 265)

We can't remember exactly how it started, but for some reason we can't stop playing fuck, marry, kill. We play with food items instead of people because it's more fun and it's a really great way to make new friends and lovers. So naturally, when Steph first heard the name of this pizza, she screamed: "This might be one of the hardest games of fuck, marry, kill!" But we'll let you be the judge of that. Bake this pie for your friends, then flip to p. 77 to play some of our all-time favorite games of fuck, marry, kill.

Before you can start building your pizza: Follow the instructions in the Stretching and Baking section (p. 73) to position the rack and preheat the oven, temper the dough, set up your pizza station, stretch the dough, and transfer it onto the pizza peel. Once those steps are complete, you're ready to build your pizza.

Top the pizza: Break the buffalo mozzarella into chunks and scatter evenly on the pizza, leaving 1½ inches of uncovered dough around the edges for the crust. Sprinkle the low-moisture mozzarella on top, avoiding the crust. Top with the torn artichokes.

Bake and rest the pizza: Follow the directions in the Stretching and Baking section (p. 73).

Finish the pizza and serve: Drape the mortadella slices over the cheese. Cut the pizza into six slices and drizzle with the pistachio pesto.

Radicchio Lardo

MAKES 1 (10-INCH) PIZZA   AUTUMN + WINTER

When Marley came back from a trip to Sicily a few years ago, he wouldn't stop begging the kitchen to make a pizza with radicchio and lardo. It's something he ate at Cave Ox, a small wine bar with an exceptional cellar that has been described by winemaker Elena Pantaleoni as the beating heart of Mount Etna. The kitchen eventually caved to Marley's request and created this pizza, adding a touch of spicy honey to balance the bitterness of the radicchio.

Before you can start building your pizza: Follow the instructions in the Stretching and Baking section (p. 73) to position the rack and preheat the oven, temper the dough, set up your pizza station, stretch the dough, and transfer it onto the pizza peel. Once those steps are complete, you're ready to build your pizza.

Dress the radicchio: In a medium bowl, combine the radicchio, olive oil, salt and pepper. Toss and massage the seasoning into the radicchio with your hands. Set aside.

Top the pizza: Distribute the garlic slices on the surface of the pizza. Break the buffalo mozzarella into small pieces with your fingers and disperse evenly, leaving 1½ inches of uncovered dough around the edges for the crust. Scatter the low-moisture mozzarella on top. Top with the dressed radicchio.

Bake and rest the pizza: Follow the directions in the Stretching and Baking section (p. 73).

Finish the pizza and serve: Immediately after the pizza comes out of the oven, top with the lardo slices and drizzle with spicy honey. Cut and serve.

1 ball Neapolitan Pizza Dough (p. 69 or 70)

2 cups roughly chopped radicchio

2 tsp extra virgin olive oil

Kosher salt

Freshly ground black pepper

½ clove garlic, thinly sliced (about 6–7 slices)

1 ball (2½ oz/75 g or about ½ cup) buffalo mozzarella

⅓ cup grated low-moisture mozzarella

6 thin slices lardo

1 tbsp Spicy Honey (p. 257)

Mr. Fun-Guy

MAKES 1 (10-INCH) PIZZA   AUTUMN

1 ball Neapolitan Pizza Dough
(p. 69 or 70)

1 clove garlic, finely minced

2 tbsp extra virgin olive oil +
more to finish

½ cup torn oyster mushrooms

½ cup sliced button mushrooms

½ cup cut or torn wild
mushrooms

½ tsp kosher salt and freshly
ground black pepper

¼ cup Taleggio Fonduta (p. 275)

2 tbsp grated Grana Padano

1 tbsp chopped fresh parsley

Flaky sea salt

Freshly ground black pepper

We firmly believe that a mushroom pizza should come with LOTS of mushrooms. Our biggest advice to recreate our Fun-Guy pie at home is *go nuts!* Buy the nicest mushrooms you can find and pile them onto your pizza high enough to throw shade on every other mushroom pizza that came before. Treat yourself.

Before you can start building your pizza: Follow the instructions in the Stretching and Baking section (p. 73) to position the rack and preheat the oven, temper the dough, set up your pizza station, stretch the dough, and transfer it onto the pizza peel. Once those steps are complete, you're ready to build your pizza.

Prepare the mushrooms: In a medium bowl, whisk together the minced garlic and olive oil. Add the mushrooms, salt and pepper and toss until the mushrooms are well coated in garlic oil. Set aside.

Top the pizza: Dollop the taleggio fonduta in the center of the pizza and, with the back of a spoon, gently spread the sauce in a circular outward motion, leaving 1½ inches of uncovered dough around the edges for the crust. Be careful not to apply too much pressure to avoid damaging the dough. Top with the dressed mushrooms.

Bake and rest the pizza: Follow the directions in the Stretching and Baking section (p. 73).

Finish the pizza and serve: Garnish the pizza with Grana Padano, chopped parsley, flaky sea salt and black pepper. Finish with a light drizzle of olive oil.

Koginut and Coppa

MAKES 1 (10-INCH) PIZZA   AUTUMN

We had this roasted squash and nduja alla pala (a Roman-style pizza made with high-hydration, long-rising dough) at Leo in Williamsburg a few years ago, so we decided to make our own version with locally grown koginut squash (a sweet and super-squashy-tasting hybrid developed by Michael Mazourek at Row 7 Seed Company). If you can't find it at your local farmers' market, you can easily replace it with buttercup or kabocha squash.

Poach the squash: Preheat the oven to 400°F. In a medium pot over medium heat, combine the squash wedges, milk, sage, nutmeg, salt and pepper. Bring to a low simmer, adjusting the heat if necessary, and cook until the squash is just becoming tender, about 10 minutes.

Bake the squash: Set up a colander over a heatproof bowl and strain the squash. Set the poaching liquid aside. Discard the sage leaves and transfer the squash to a parchment paper–lined baking sheet. Bake in the oven until the surface of the squash has dried up a bit and the flesh is tender, about 15 minutes. Set aside and let it cool down.

Make the squash bechamel: In another pot, melt the butter over medium heat. Add the flour, stirring constantly, until the mixture takes on a light golden color. Whisk in the squash poaching liquid. Reduce the heat and whisk continually until the liquid thickens slightly, 5–8 minutes. Taste and adjust the seasoning with salt and pepper. Set aside to cool. Note that you will need only ¼ cup of this bechamel for your pizza. You can use the rest to make a simple gratin, lasagna or cannelloni, or turn it into a delicious mac and cheese sauce by adding extra cheese.

(continued)

Squash + Bechamel
¼ koginut or buttercup squash, peeled and cut into wedges

2 cups whole milk

5 leaves fresh sage

½ tsp freshly grated nutmeg

3 pinches kosher salt

A few twists of freshly ground black pepper

1 tbsp unsalted butter

1 tbsp all-purpose flour

Pizza
1 ball Neapolitan Pizza Dough (p. 69 or 70)

3 slices provolone

½ shallot, thinly sliced

½ cup Stracciatella (p. 271)

Flaky sea salt

Freshly ground black pepper

6 slices (about 3 oz/90 g) spicy coppa

Extra virgin olive oil

Before you can start building your pizza: Follow the instructions in the Stretching and Baking section (p. 73) to position the rack and preheat the oven, temper the dough, set up your pizza station, stretch the dough, and transfer it onto the pizza peel. Once those steps are complete, you're ready to build your pizza.

Sauce the pizza: Dollop ¼ cup bechamel sauce in the center of the pizza and, with the back of a spoon, gently spread it in a circular outward motion, leaving 1½ inches of uncovered dough around the edges for the crust. Be careful not to apply too much pressure to avoid damaging the dough.

Top the pizza: Disperse the provolone slices evenly on the surface of the dough. Break the squash into chunks with your hands and scatter them over the cheese slices. Top everything with the shallots.

Bake and rest the pizza: Follow the directions in the Stretching and Baking section (p. 73).

Finish the pizza and serve: Cut the pizza into six slices, dollop stracciatella on each slice and season with flaky sea salt and pepper. Carefully drape the coppa slices over each slice. Drizzle with extra virgin olive oil and serve.

Biancaroni

IYKYK. This is the original off-menu item inspired by a pizza Chris saw on the list at Paulie Gee's in Brooklyn. At its core, it's a white version of our Diavolo 2.0, but with extra honey and basil. Even though it might be one of our all-time favorite pies, we've always kept this pizza secret for some reason (at this point, we might need to have an intervention just to talk about the length of the shadow menu at Elena).

1 ball Neapolitan Pizza Dough (p. 69 or 70)

1 clove garlic, thinly sliced

1 ball (2½ oz/75 g or about ½ cup) buffalo mozzarella

¼ cup grated auricchio (spicy provolone)

2 oz (60 g) cup thinly sliced salami

1 tsp Spicy Honey (p. 257)

2 tbsp Pepperoncini (p. 286)

6–8 leaves fresh basil

Before you can start building your pizza: Follow the instructions in the Stretching and Baking section (p. 73) to position the rack and preheat the oven, temper the dough, set up your pizza station, stretch the dough, and transfer it onto the pizza peel. Once those steps are complete, you're ready to build your pizza.

Top the pizza: Spread the garlic slices evenly on the surface of the pizza. Break the buffalo mozzarella into chunks and disperse them over the garlic slices, leaving 1½ inches of uncovered dough around the edges for the crust. Sprinkle the grated auricchio all over the pizza, making sure to avoid the crust. Top with the slices of salami.

Bake and rest the pizza: Follow the directions in the Stretching and Baking section (p. 73).

Finish the pizza and serve: Cut the pizza into six slices, drizzle it with spicy honey and finish with pepperoncini and basil leaves.

Kevin McCallister

A whole cheese pizza just for you! Inspired by the cheese pizza Kevin McCallister gets delivered in the '90s classic movie *Home Alone*, this pizza became a staple during the first COVID lockdown when we were ironically home alone. It's the perfect comfort pizza to eat by yourself and it's also perfect for a bunch of kids to share.

1 ball Neapolitan Pizza Dough (p. 69 or 70)
⅓ cup crushed tomatoes
¾ cup grated low-moisture mozzarella

Before you can start building your pizza: Follow the instructions in the Stretching and Baking section (p. 73) to position the rack and preheat the oven, temper the dough, set up your pizza station, stretch the dough, and transfer it onto the pizza peel. Once those steps are complete, you're ready to build your pizza.

Sauce the pizza: Dollop the crushed tomatoes in the center of the pizza and, with the back of a spoon, gently spread the sauce in a circular outward motion, leaving 1½ inches of uncovered dough around the edges for the crust. Be careful not to apply too much pressure to avoid damaging the dough.

Top the pizza: Sprinkle the low-moisture mozzarella evenly on top of the sauce, avoiding the crust area.

Bake and rest the pizza: Follow the directions in the Stretching and Baking section (p. 73).

Finish the pizza and serve: Cut the pizza into six slices and let the kids (or your inner child) go wild.

PIZZA PEOPLE

The world is filled with chefs who have dedicated their lives to working with dough and fresh ingredients, all in the name of pizza. We affectionately call these peculiar creatures pizza people. Here are a few of the ones who have inspired us over the years, and places you should check out.

Pizzeria Bianco

Bianco is considered by many to be one of the best pizzerias in the United States. Before we opened Elena, our good friend Riad Nasr (Frenchette, Le Rock) suggested that Emma spend a few days learning how to make pizza with the man himself in Phoenix, Arizona. Turns out that Chris Bianco is not only a master pizzaiolo but also one of the sweetest men ever. He and his friend Rob DiNapoli also have their own brand of canned tomatoes called Bianco DiNapoli, which we use on all of our red pizzas (as should you).

Pizzeria Bianco—multiple locations in Phoenix and Los Angeles

Ops and Leo

Splitting his time between Ops and Leo, Mike Fadem makes some of the best pizza in the world. Anyone who has been lucky enough to eat at either one of his Brooklyn restaurants knows that to be true. The first time Ryan ate at Ops in 2017, he left in shock. Not only was the pizza incredible (the rojo pie with mortadella and peppers still haunts his dreams), but it also left him feeling light, even after he devoured at least three entire pies. Following that experience, making pizza that tasted great, but also made people feel good, became one of our guiding principles.

Ops—346 Himrod St., Brooklyn
Leo—123 Havemeyer St., Brooklyn

Roberta's

Going to Roberta's when it first opened felt like you were being let in on one of the city's best-kept pizza secrets. At the time, Bushwick was this off-the-beaten-path neighborhood where you didn't expect to find much. But once you were seated at one of the large communal tables, you felt right at home. That's a feeling we've tried to recreate with our restaurants by picking unusual locations (like a former strip club or a pretty unremarkable box-shaped building behind a hardware store) and making the interior feel super special—like you've just stumbled upon a hidden treasure no one knows about yet.

Roberta's—multiple locations in Brooklyn, Manhattan and Los Angeles

L'Industrie

Chef Massimo Laveglia has managed to reinvent and elevate the classic New York slice shop by making pizza using only fresh, high-quality ingredients. We enjoyed what L'Industrie was doing so much following our first visit that we named one of our alla pala pizzas (a longer-style pizza typically served on a paddle) after their shop. Inspired by L'Industrie's signature burrata pizza, we make ours with fresh stracciatella and anchovies.

L'Industrie—254 S 2nd St., Brooklyn

Bonci

Gabriele Bonci is the all-time heavyweight pizza champion. The depth of flavor, crispiness, chewiness and airiness of his dough, along with the quality of the ingredients and the combination of toppings he uses, are unparalleled. Every time we eat at Bonci, we're reminded of the true meaning of pizza. It's a mind-altering experience.

Bonci Pizzarium—Via della Meloria 43, Rome
Panifico Bonci—Via Trionfale 36, Rome

Mattachioni

We owe a lot to Dave Mattachioni. His recipes and techniques were a touchstone when we were embarking on our pizza odyssey. Not only has he been quietly making some of the best pizza in Toronto for years, but Dave also rocks Tobias Fünke–style denim short shorts when the weather gets hot. What's not to love?

Mattachioni—1617 Dupont St., Toronto

Lovely's Fifty Fifty

We love Sarah Minnick's local and seasonal approach to making pizza in a colder climate. She doesn't let anything get in her way. At her small wood-fire pizza restaurant in Portland, she mixes her sourdough pies using a variety of local artisanal flours and sources every single one of her vegetable toppings in Oregon.

Lovely's Fifty Fifty—4039 N Mississippi Ave., Portland

Pam Yung

Our friend Pam Yung is a free spirit with a passion and incomparable talent for pizza, which is why she is the only person on this list who is not tied to a specific restaurant. We first met Pam when she was the pastry chef at Roberta's, but since then she's operated her own restaurant (the now-defunct Semilla in Brooklyn) and worked all over the world, including Flor in London and a pizza residency at Blue Hill. Her skills, humility and openness have always been an inspiration to us—so much so that we would follow her to the end of the earth.

@wandrlstng on Instagram

Naturally Leavened al Taglio Pizza Dough

MAKES ENOUGH DOUGH FOR 2 AL TAGLIO PIZZAS

Special Equipment
Mixer (optional)
Very large mixing bowl
Dough scraper

6⅓ cups (820 g) bread flour

1⅓ cups (200 g) spelt or whole wheat flour

3 cups (750 ml) water, room temperature

1 cup (200 g) Sourdough Starter (p. 67)

5 tsp (25 g) fine sea salt

3 tbsp (45 ml) extra virgin olive oil, divided, + more oil or butter for greasing the baking sheets

Semolina rimacinata or all-purpose flour, to dust your work surface

Al taglio is a rectangular style of pizza that's cooked on a baking sheet and typically sold in square slices by weight. Whenever we go to Italy, one of our first stops is always Bonci Pizzarium in Rome, where they sell all sorts of al taglio pies, from stracciatella with marinated zucchini to tripes cacio e pepe. Al taglio is deceptively easy to make at home and can feed a lot of people. And when it's done right, the dough rises to form Instagram-worthy air bubbles that are hard to resist.

Hydrate the flours: In the bowl of a stand mixer with a hook attachment (or in a very large bowl using a rubber spatula), combine the flours with the water. Mix on the lowest setting until a shaggy mass forms. Turn off the mixer and let it rest for 10 minutes.

Mix or knead the dough: Add the sourdough starter and salt and continue to knead until the dough is smooth and relatively uniform, about 10 minutes. Transfer the dough to a clean surface and scrape out the mixing bowl using a dough scraper, discarding any dried bits. Generously oil that same bowl with 2 tbsp olive oil and place the dough inside. Cover the dough and rest it at room temperature for 30 minutes.

Fold the dough and let it rise: Starting with the edge farthest away from you, gently lift and fold the dough in half over itself. (This motion should be done confidently to stretch the dough without ever tearing it.) Rotate the bowl 90 degrees and repeat the same process until the dough has been folded on itself for a total of four times, rotating the bowl after each fold. Cover the dough and rest it at room temperature for 30 minutes. Repeat the folding process two more times, resting the dough 30 minutes at the end of each folding session. The whole process should take about 1½ hours.

Divide the dough: Transfer the dough to a lightly floured surface by flipping the bowl over and letting the dough slowly fall out. Using a dough scraper, divide the dough in half.

Shape the dough: Working with one piece at a time, fold each corner toward the center of the dough. Then fold the dough on itself twice as if you were folding a piece of paper to put in an envelope. Use the dough scraper to tuck the edges and create a smooth and even oval shape. Put the dough back in the same oiled container. Cover and chill in the fridge for 2 days. During this time, the dough should proof gently, becoming lighter and springier to the touch. It can be stored in a lightly oiled, sealed container in the fridge for up to 3 days or frozen for a few months.

When you are ready to make your pizza, proof the dough again: Grease two baking sheets with olive oil (or use butter for an extra-crispy bottom crust). Uncover the dough and coat lightly with 1 tbsp olive oil. Carefully transfer each dough portion onto the baking sheets, keeping the top side of the proofed dough facing up. Using your fingertips, gently press down on the surface of the dough to release some of the air. Cover with a damp towel and let it rest in a warm spot for at least 30 minutes and up to 3 hours. (The longer the dough proofs, the more relaxed it will become, making it easier to stretch but also more fragile.)

Stretch the dough: Once the dough has proofed, uncover it and start stretching it by lifting it from the bottom to make sure no air gets trapped underneath. Gradually and gently stretch out the corners of the dough toward the edges of the baking sheet. Continue working with your fingertips to stretch the dough until it's about the same size as the baking sheet. Press the dough firmly into the corners. Repeat this process with the remaining portion of dough. Your al taglio is now ready to welcome toppings.

Yeasted al Taglio Pizza Dough

MAKES ENOUGH DOUGH FOR 2 AL TAGLIO PIZZAS

Special Equipment
Mixer (optional)
Very large mixing bowl
Dough scraper

7 cups + 3 tbsp (934 g) bread flour

⅔ cup + 2 tbsp (110 g) spelt or whole wheat flour

1 packet (8 g) active dry yeast

3 tbsp (45 ml) extra virgin olive oil, divided, + more oil or butter for greasing the baking sheets

3 cups (750 ml) water, room temperature

2 tbsp (32 g) fine sea salt

Semolina rimacinata or all-purpose flour, to dust your work surface

This is the yeasted version of our al taglio dough. If you have made the naturally leavened dough before, make sure to read this recipe thoroughly, as some of the directions deviate from the naturally leavened version.

Mix the dough: In the bowl of a stand mixer with a hook attachment (or in a very large bowl using a rubber spatula), combine the flours and the yeast. Add 1 tbsp olive oil and the water. Mix on the lowest setting until a shaggy mass forms. Turn off the mixer and let it rest for 10 minutes.

Mix or knead the dough: Add the salt and continue to knead until the dough is smooth and relatively uniform, about 10 minutes. Transfer the dough to a clean surface and scrape out the mixing bowl using a dough scraper, discarding any dried bits. Generously oil that same bowl with 2 tbsp olive oil and place the dough inside. Cover the dough and rest it at room temperature for 30 minutes.

Fold the dough and let it rise overnight: Starting with the edge farthest away from you, gently lift up and fold the dough in half over itself. (This motion should be done confidently to stretch the dough without ever tearing it.) Rotate the bowl 90 degrees and repeat the same process until the dough has been folded on itself for a total of four times, rotating the bowl after each fold. Cover the dough and rest it at room temperature for 30 minutes. Repeat the folding process two more times, resting the dough 30 minutes at the end of each folding session. The whole process should take about 1½ hours. Cover the dough and let it ferment in the fridge for at least 12 hours and up to 3 days. The dough should roughly double in size during that time.

Divide the dough: Transfer the dough to a lightly floured surface by flipping the bowl over and letting the dough slowly fall out. Using a dough scraper, divide the dough in half.

Shape the dough: Working with one piece at a time, fold each corner toward the center of the dough. Then fold the dough on itself twice as if you were folding a piece of paper to put in an envelope. Use the dough scraper to tuck the edges and create a smooth and even oval shape. Put the dough back in the same oiled container, seam down. Cover and chill in the fridge for 1 day. During this time, the dough should proof gently, becoming lighter and springier to the touch. The blobs can be stored in a lightly oiled, sealed container in the fridge for up to 3 days or frozen for a few months.

Proof the dough again: Grease two baking sheets with olive oil (or use butter for an extra-crispy bottom crust). Uncover the dough and coat lightly in olive oil. Carefully transfer each dough ball onto the baking sheets, keeping the top side of the proofed dough facing up. Using your fingertips, gently press down on the surface of dough to release some of the air. Cover with a damp towel and let it rest in a warm spot until the dough has doubled in size and become very supple, about 2–3 hours. (Note that the longer the dough proofs, the easier it will be to stretch, but it will also be more fragile.)

Stretch the dough: Once the dough has proofed, uncover it and start stretching it by lifting it from the bottom to make sure no air gets trapped underneath. Gradually and gently stretch out the corners of the dough toward the edges of the baking sheet. Continue working with your fingertips to stretch the dough until it's about the same size as the baking sheet. Press the dough firmly into the corners. Repeat this process with the remaining ball of dough. Your al taglio is now ready to welcome toppings.

Rossa

½ recipe Al Taglio Pizza Dough (enough for one pizza) (p. 104 or 106)

2 cups crushed tomatoes

2–3 cloves garlic, thinly sliced

2 pinches crushed dried Espelette peppers

2 pinches dried oregano (Sicilian if possible)

Extra virgin olive oil

Flaky sea salt

1 cup Stracciatella (p. 271; optional, but should be seriously considered)

Cantabrian anchovies, to your liking (optional)

The rossa is the number-one choice of true pizza aficionados because there is nowhere to hide. The dough has to be proofed just right, the sauce has to be great and the pizza has to be baked perfectly. It is pizza in its purest form and can be as profoundly flavorful as any other slice. Pro tip: take your rossa to the next level by adding a few Cantabrian anchovies. You'll thank us later.

Preheat the oven: Place a rack in the upper and lower thirds of the oven. Preheat the oven to 500°F.

Stretch the dough: Once your dough is done proofing and you are ready to make your pizza, stretch it as directed in the al taglio dough recipe (p. 104 or 106).

Top the pizza: Dollop the crushed tomatoes in the center of the pizza and, with the back of a spoon, gently spread the sauce in a back-and-forth motion, almost to the edge of the crust. Scatter the garlic slices all over the surface of the al taglio. Top with the crushed Espelette peppers and dried oregano. Drizzle with olive oil.

Bake the pizza: Bake the pizza on the bottom rack, moving it to the top rack halfway through, until the crust is golden brown, 12–15 minutes.

Finish the pizza and serve: Add a drizzle of olive oil, sprinkle with flaky sea salt and top with Stracciatella and Cantabrian anchovies (both optional). Cut into squares like the Romans do.

Ode to Ops

MAKES 1 (12 × 15-INCH) PIZZA   SPRING

Ops is a small pizza restaurant in Brooklyn that serves wood-fire pies and natural wines (great concept). As the owner, our good friend Mike Fadem, would humbly say: "We do what we do." Their cicero, packed with onions, sharp provolone and mozzarella, is spectacular in its simplicity and the way it manages to elevate an ingredient as humble as the onion. This is our ode to that pizza.

Preheat the oven: Place a rack in the upper and lower thirds of the oven. Preheat the oven to 500°F.

Stretch the dough: Once your dough is done proofing and you are ready to make your pizza, stretch it as directed in the al taglio dough recipe (p. 104 or 106).

Top the pizza: Scatter the provolone slices over the pizza. Top with the diced onions and mozzarella. Add a drizzle of olive oil and season with a generous pinch of salt.

Bake the pizza: Bake the pizza on the bottom rack, moving it to the top rack halfway through, until the crust is golden brown and the onions are charred in spots, 12–15 minutes.

Finish the pizza and serve: Drizzle the pizza with more olive oil and season with flaky sea salt and black pepper.

½ recipe Al Taglio Pizza Dough (enough for one pizza) (p. 104 or 106)

5 oz (142 g) aged provolone, thinly sliced

4 cups diced onions, about ½ inch (preferably a mix of varieties)

1½ cups grated low-moisture mozzarella

Extra virgin olive oil

Flaky sea salt

Freshly ground black pepper

Passion Patates

MAKES 1 (12 × 15-INCH) PIZZA   FALL + WINTER

½ recipe Al Taglio Pizza Dough (enough for one pizza) (p. 104 or 106)

1 lb (450 g) fingerling potatoes or 2 large Yukon gold potatoes, scrubbed

6 fresh rosemary sprigs (2 whole and 4 chopped), divided

1 tsp black peppercorns

Extra virgin olive oil

5 oz (142 g) smoked provolone or smoked cheddar, sliced

2 balls (5.2 oz/150 g or about 1 cup) buffalo mozzarella

1 small yellow onion, thinly sliced (about 1 cup)

Freshly ground black pepper

1 cup finely grated parmesan

Potato pizza makes our knees weak and our hearts melt. Biting into a thick layer of rosemary-infused potatoes, cheese and dough feels like getting tucked into bed and kissed on the forehead by a loved one. It's pure comfort.

Temper the dough: If your dough is in the fridge, remove it and let it temper while you cook the potatoes. If it's still proofing on the counter, leave it there.

Cook the potatoes: Bring a pot of salted water to a boil. Add the potatoes, two rosemary sprigs and the peppercorns and simmer until the potatoes are fork-tender but not falling apart, 20 minutes for fingerlings and 25–35 for larger potatoes. Remove the potatoes from the pot and let them rest for a few minutes. Once they are cool enough to handle but still warm, peel the skins off using a small paring knife. Put the potatoes in a bowl and break them into rough chunks. Add 2 tbsp olive oil and toss to coat.

Preheat the oven: Place a rack in the upper and lower thirds of the oven. Preheat the oven to 500°F.

Stretch the dough: Once your dough is done proofing and you are ready to make your pizza, stretch it as directed in the al taglio dough recipe (p. 104 or 106).

Top the pizza: Distribute the provolone on the pizza, reaching as close to the edges as possible. Break the buffalo mozzarella into small pieces and disperse evenly. Top with the crushed potatoes, sliced onions and chopped rosemary.

Bake the pizza: Place the pizza on the bottom rack, moving it to the top halfway through, and bake until the crust is golden brown and the onions are charred in spots, 12–15 minutes.

Finish the pizza and serve: Garnish with more olive oil, freshly ground black pepper and freshly grated parmesan. Cut into squares and enjoy!

Sausage and Peppers

MAKES 1 (12 × 15-INCH) PIZZA   SUMMER

This pizza is loosely inspired by the sausage, pepper and onion hero sandwiches from *The Sopranos*. Sausage and peppers are a classic American Italian combination because they taste incredible together (spicy, sweet and fatty). We strongly recommend preparing a double batch of the sausage to make hoagies the next day (p. 214).

Roast and steam the peppers: Preheat the oven to 450°F and line a baking sheet with parchment paper. Place the peppers on the baking sheet and coat them lightly with 1 tsp olive oil. Bake until the peppers are charred around the edges, turning them halfway, about 20 minutes. Place the peppers inside a covered container to cool and steam for 30 minutes.

Make the fennel sausage mix: In a large bowl, toss to combine the red wine, kosher salt, brown sugar, garlic powder, onion powder, toasted fennel seeds, smoked paprika and dried chili flakes. Add the ground pork and, working with your hands, mix until the meat is fully combined with all the spices. Make sure not to overwork the meat—you want it to hold its shape without becoming too stiff. Do a taste test by heating a glug of olive oil in a small frying pan over medium-high heat and cooking a small chunk of the sausage mix. Adjust the seasoning with salt and pepper if needed. Set aside.

Marinate the peppers: When the peppers feel cool enough to handle, remove the skins, cores, seeds and stems. Slice the peppers into ½-inch-wide strips. In a medium bowl, combine the roasted peppers with the red wine vinegar, parsley, capers, sugar, remaining olive oil, salt, garlic and chili flakes. Toss to combine, cover and set aside. The marinated peppers will keep in an airtight container in the fridge for up to 2 weeks.

Preheat the oven: Place a rack in the upper and lower thirds of the oven. Preheat the oven to 500°F.

(continued)

Marinated peppers

3 red bell peppers

1½ tbsp extra virgin olive oil, divided

2 tbsp red wine vinegar

2 tbsp chopped fresh parsley

2 tbsp capers

1½ tsp sugar

¾ tsp kosher salt

1 clove garlic, finely minced

½ tsp dried chili flakes (optional)

Fennel sausage

1 tbsp red wine

½ tsp kosher salt + more if needed

¾ tsp brown sugar

¼ tsp garlic powder

½ tsp onion powder

1¼ tsp toasted fennel seeds

½ tbsp smoked paprika (we like La Dalia)

¼ tsp dried chili flakes

½ lb (225 g) ground pork shoulder (ideally a meat-to-fat ratio of 75:25)

Freshly ground black pepper (optional)

Assembly

½ recipe Al Taglio Pizza Dough (enough for one pizza) (p. 104 or 106)

1 cup crushed tomatoes

2–3 cloves garlic, thinly sliced

½ tsp dried oregano

5 oz (142 g) aged provolone, sliced

1½ cups grated low-moisture mozzarella

½ cup chopped onions

Extra virgin olive oil

Flaky sea salt

Freshly ground black pepper

Stretch the dough: Once your dough is done proofing and you are ready to make your pizza, stretch it as directed in the al taglio dough recipe (p. 104 or 106).

Top the pizza: Dollop the crushed tomatoes in the center of the pizza and, with the back of a spoon, gently spread the sauce in a back-and-forth motion, almost to the edge of the crust. Scatter the garlic slices and dried oregano all over the surface of the pizza. Evenly distribute the aged provolone, reaching as close to the edges as possible. Disperse the grated mozzarella and top with the onions, raw sausage bits no bigger than a quarter, and marinated peppers.

Bake the pizza: Bake the pizza on the bottom rack, moving it to the top rack halfway through, until the crust is golden brown and the onions are charred in spots, 12–15 minutes.

Finish the pizza and serve: Drizzle the pizza with more olive oil and season with flaky sea salt and black pepper.

NATURAL WINE ALL THE TIME

By Ryan Gray

In the spring of 2011, I was about to open my first Italian restaurant, Nora Gray, and I knew nothing about Italian wine. I had spent the previous five years buying, selling and excessively drinking the most noble wines from Burgundy, Bordeaux and the Loire. I was also really into Beaujolais, Jura and Roussillon wines. As for Italy, I was aware of the most prestigious Super Tuscans and could tell you the basic differences between a Barolo and a Brunello. The rest was kind of a mystery.

A few years prior, I had been introduced to the work of winemakers like Arianna Occhipinti, and Radikon. Even if I didn't quite understand the wines, I just couldn't get enough of them. Nobody used the term "natural wine" back then, but there was something palpably alive about these wines that made them stand out to me. I was hooked. I knew in that moment that I wanted to make these low-intervention, biodynamic, low- or no-sulfur wines the focus of the wine program at my restaurants.

My Italian natural wine education grew from these winemakers. These wines have helped shape my palate and ethos as a buyer and restaurateur. They have also become the backbone of my wine programs at Nora Gray, Elena and Gia. Over the years, I have hosted, visited and befriended these winemakers, as well as many other groundbreaking, passionate and intoxicating vignerons. Here are a few others that are really important to us at Elena.

La Stoppa

We named our restaurant after winemaker Elena Pantaleoni because she's generous, funny, wise and uncompromising in her vision—even when that means making difficult, not-so-obvious business decisions. When she inherited her family's winery in Emilia-Romagna after her father passed away, she ripped out popular vines of Pinot Noir and Cabernet Sauvignon to plant indigenous varietals like Barbera, Malvasia and Bonarda. She wanted to make wines that truly represented and highlighted her region, instead of those that were commercially appealing. She represents the ideal of what we wanted the restaurant to live up to. She leads from the heart and sees herself as someone who has the privilege and the position to make things better, and so she does. When she first visited the restaurant, she said something that stuck with us and reflected how we felt before we opened Elena: "After so many years, if you're still stressed, it means there's something wrong." It's that kind of thinking that continues to drive us to create positive change around us.

Pacina

Tucked in the picturesque hills of Tuscany, Pacina is our favorite place in the world. It's hard to put into words what being at Pacina is like, other than saying that it feels like you've arrived. When you're standing in the field overlooking the vineyard, olive groves and chickpea patches, it's like you're meeting Mother Nature for the first time. There is a life force emanating from that place that is palpable. The winemakers, Giovanna Tiezzi and Stefano Borsa, also happen to be some of the most lovable and passionate people we've ever met (and so are their children, Maria and Carlo). We even named our newest restaurant, Gia, in honor of Giovanna, who often talks about how as winemakers, they are essentially midwives who facilitate the process between vine and bottle. The vines and the grapes were there long before them and will continue to be there long after they're gone.

La Villana

We love Joy Kull not only because she has a sparkling personality and makes amazing wine, but also because she's living the life we all wish we had. As an American who moved to Italy to make wine at the cult natural winery Le Coste, Joy fell in love with a shepherd and now runs her own winery near Lake Bolsena, a volcanic crater lake in one of Italy's most underappreciated regions. Her wines are predominantly made from Sangiovese and Procanico (a local clone of Trebbiano), but don't sleep on her Aleatico or Moscato if you can find them. Several Elena staffers have worked harvest at La Villana, which resulted in a special Elena cuvée called "Pizza Wine". It is a blend of Sangiovese and Merlot grapes and—you guessed it—pairs incredibly well with pizza.

De Fermo

Having no background in winemaking, Stefano Papetti nonetheless grew up obsessed with natural wines. His wife would often talk about this piece of land that her family owned in Abruzzo, and when she finally showed it to him, Stefano's life changed forever. The property was thick with pristine, organically farmed old vines, and even had a winery that had been abandoned during WWII. Slowly, Stefano started making wine and growing grains, olives, legumes and vegetables. And so, De Fermo was born. In 2018, Marley worked harvest at the winery, where he footstomped our first Italian wine collaboration, a dark rosé made with Montepulciano grapes aged in a ceramic egg. The wine is amazing, but we especially love the label, which features such a stupid photo of Marley as a kid that it made Steph cry with laughter the first time she saw it.

Cascina degli Ulivi

Winemaker Stefano Bellotti, who passed away in 2018, was considered by many to be the godfather of the natural wine movement in Italy. He was a rebel at heart, always working outside the appellation system, and the king of biodynamic agriculture (a holistic type of organic agriculture that is part farming, part spiritual practice: it follows the lunar cycle and views the vineyard as a living organism where the earth, plants, animals and insects are all working together). The winery doubles as a self-sustaining farm where they raise milk cows and grow wheat with which they make everything from bread to pasta. A lot of people come work at Cascina degli Ulivi specifically to learn about biodynamics and polyculture—about the kind of farming we need to see more of in the world.

Cantina Giardino

Cantina Giardino is located in a remote part of Italy where you'd probably never venture unless you were going to visit them, about an hour and a half east of Naples in a town called Ariano Irpino. They have vineyards scattered around the winery and throughout the region, where they tend to ancient vines of indigenous varietals like Aglianico, Greco Di Tufo and Coda di Volpe. They have a very hands-off approach to winemaking that results in some of the wildest wines we've ever tasted. It's all about letting the grapes do their thing and trusting that it's all going to work out, which it almost always does. The area benefits from cool nights and warm days, which give the wines the opportunity to ripen perfectly while retaining some structure and acidity.

Podere Santa Marie

Luisa and Marino Colleoni became accidental winemakers when they found vines buried under brush while taking a walk around a property they had recently purchased in Montalcino,

a region famous for producing prestigious Brunello wines. When people think of Brunello di Montalcino, they often think of expensive and highly stylized wines. The Colleonis' wines are not like that. They're delicate, sexy and frankly super interesting for the region. The couple has an amazing amount of respect for the land and the vines. They work with minimal intervention to let the story of each vintage be told, unedited.

Les Pervenches

Initially, we thought we'd keep this list 100 percent Italian, but because Elena has always been this beautiful combination of Italian dishes made with Quebec ingredients, we'd be remiss not to talk about the wines made right here in our backyard by our friends Véronique Hupin and Mike Marler at Les Pervenches. Before them, nobody thought varietals like Chardonnay, Pinot Gris or Pinot Noir could survive our freezing winters or manage to ripen during our all-too-short summers. Yet Mike and Véro make what we think are some of the best wines in Canada—maybe even North America. They have proved that old-world grapes can not only thrive in Quebec, but also produce wines that can rival some of the best Europe has to offer (and they keep it all natural). Every year, we make a cuvée with them called CHINGÓN, which is basically our version of a Brutal. Plus, because they are the nicest and kindest people around, they also let us use their outdoor pizza oven whenever we come over.

VINO ROSSO

PASTA

Making fresh pasta is not as daunting and messy as most people think—the process is in fact quite simple and therapeutic.* Pasta is essentially just flour and some kind of liquid, whether that's eggs, water or puree. Once you've gathered your ingredients (more on why you should consider freshly milled flour and farm-fresh eggs on pp. 11 and 12), there's really not a lot to stress about.

That's why whenever life comes at us too fast, we like to take a deep breath and slowly start to incorporate flour into freshly separated egg yolks. Then we knead the shaggy ball of dough with our bare hands, feeling its texture and elasticity change as the flour hydrates. Just for a moment, we forget all about our worries as we gently feed a chunk of brightly colored egg dough into a pasta roller and watch it stretch a little longer and thinner with every passing moment.

We'll save you from having to endure our speech on the relaxing properties of shaping farfalle or caramelle. Just trust us. Put on your favorite record, tuck your last two brain cells into bed and let your hands do the work. Next thing you know, you'll be sitting in front of a comforting bowl of fresh Tagliatelle with Rosemary Sugo (p. 163), unable to recall what worried you in the first place and why you ever thought making fresh pasta was out of your grasp.

* Disclaimer: pasta making should never serve as a replacement for actual therapy.

Semolina Pasta Dough

SERVES 4–6 (MAKES 1⅓ LB DOUGH)

Special Equipment
Food processor
Pasta roller
Blender (for the Green Semolina
Pasta Dough)

3½ cups semolina rimacinata
1 cup water, divided

Semolina dough is used to make the kind of dried extruded pasta that was historically manufactured in Southern Italy (like the ones you find in boxes at the grocery store), short, hand-shaped pasta and simple rolled noodles. A simple mix of water and semolina rimacinata (a sandy yellow flour made from hard durum wheat), it is stiffer and has more bite than its egg-based counterpart. This is our basic recipe for semolina dough, which you can riff on by swapping some of the water with various liquids or vegetable purees to achieve different flavor profiles.

Make the dough: Place the flour in a food processor, and while the motor is running, slowly add ¾ cup water [1]. You should notice the dough starting to stick to the wall of the food processor [2]. Pulse a few more seconds until the mixture begins to look crumbly. Transfer the dough to a bowl and start tossing and breaking it up with your hands to even out the moisture and consistency [3]. At this point, the dough should feel like wet sand and hold together when squeezed, not crumble.

Return the dough to the food processor and pulse again, slowly adding the remaining ¼ cup water, as needed. You want the dough to look even and hold its shape when squeezed. Put the dough back into the bowl and, using your hands, press and form the dough into a thick disk [4]. Wrap it using reusable food wrap or store it in a tight-fitting container to protect it from drying out. Rest the dough at room temperature for at least 30 minutes before shaping it.

Green Semolina Pasta Dough

Puree the spinach: Bring a medium pot of salted water to a boil. Prepare a bowl of ice water. Add the spinach and blanch until wilted but not mushy, about 1 minute. Transfer the spinach to the ice bath to stop it from cooking any further. Squeeze the spinach to drain it, then chop it roughly. You should have about ¾ cup blanched, chopped spinach. Transfer the spinach to a blender, add 3 tsp water and blend until pureed.

Make the spinach pasta dough: Follow the instructions for the semolina pasta dough on page 124, using 4 cups semolina rimacinata (instead of 3½ cups), and replacing the 1 cup water with the spinach puree and ¼ cup water, as needed, when returning the dough to the food processor. Make sure to let your dough rest for at least 30 minutes before rolling.

8 cups raw spinach
3 tsp + ¼ cup water, divided
4 cups semolina rimacinata

(continued)

Red Wine Semolina Pasta Dough

2½ cups semolina rimacinata
½ cup reduced red wine (p. 149)
2 tbsp water

Make the dough: Follow the instructions for the semolina pasta dough on page 124, using 2½ cups semolina rimacinata (instead of 3½ cups) and adding ½ cup reduced red wine, along with the water, as needed, when returning the dough to the food processor. Make sure to let your dough rest for at least 30 minutes before rolling.

Flour and Semolina Pasta Dough

1 cup all-purpose flour
1 cup semolina rimacinata
1 cup whole wheat or spelt flour
1 cup water
1 tsp extra virgin olive oil

Mix the dough: In a large bowl, whisk to combine the all-purpose, semolina rimacinata and whole wheat flours. In a small bowl, combine the water and the olive oil. Pour the flour mixture onto a clean surface. With your hands, carefully shape the flour into a well large enough to accommodate the water and the olive oil. Pour the water and oil mixture into the flour well. Using a fork, slowly incorporate the flour with the liquid, beating gently until it becomes a messy paste. Combine the last bits of flour using your hands. If the dough is too dry, add a bit of water, preferably using a spray bottle or a measuring cup to control the flow.

Once the dough looks ragged, scrape the shaggy bits from your hands with your fingers and use the sticky parts of the dough to pick up leftover bits on the counter, scraping the surface with a butter knife or a bench scraper as you go. Some drier bits might be beyond saving. Simply scrape them off and discard.

Knead and rest the dough: Knead the dough by hand until the consistency becomes more or less regular, 5–10 minutes. If you get tired, do this in two steps, making sure to cover the dough with a damp towel, food wrap or a bowl flipped upside down to prevent it drying out while you take a break. As the dough rests, the gluten will relax, making it much easier to work with.

Once the dough is even, wrap it and rest it at room temperature for at least 1 hour, after which it should be smooth and tender enough to take an imprint when poked, but stiff enough that it takes a bit of force to press down. There shouldn't be any dry flour bits, but if there are, simply spritz the dough with a bit of water. Rest it, wrapped, for another 10 minutes before rolling.

Egg Pasta Dough

SERVES 4–6 (MAKES 1¼ LB DOUGH)

Thanks to the fat content of the egg yolks and the olive oil, this dough has a richer and suppler texture than semolina dough, making it the ideal choice for more complicated shapes, such as folded and stuffed pasta. This is our master egg dough recipe, but you can play around with it by changing some of the flours to create different flavors and textures.

Separate the eggs: In a small bowl, crack and separate the eggs (save the egg whites to make the Pistachio Cookies on p. 231 or the Suppli on p. 151), and add the whole egg and 1 tsp olive oil to the five yolks.

Mix the dough: Pour the flour onto a clean surface. With your hands, carefully shape the flour into a well with a hole large enough to accommodate all the eggs [1]. Place the egg mixture into the flour well [2]. Using a fork, slowly incorporate the flour into the egg mixture, beating gently until it becomes a messy paste [3]. Combine the last bits of flour using your hands [4]. If the dough is too dry, add a bit of water, preferably using a spray bottle or a measuring cup to control the flow.

Once the dough looks ragged, scrape the shaggy bits from your hands with your fingers and use the sticky parts of the dough to pick up leftover bits on the counter, scraping the surface with a butter knife or a bench scraper as you go. Some drier bits might be beyond saving. Simply scrape off and discard.

Knead and rest the dough: Knead the dough by hand [5] until the consistency becomes more or less regular [6], 5–10 minutes. If you get tired, do this in two steps, making sure to cover the dough with a damp towel, food wrap or a bowl flipped upside down to prevent it drying out while you take a break. As the dough rests, the gluten will relax, making it much easier to work with. If you are very strong (or have a friend willing to take a shift), do it all in one go.

(continued)

Special Equipment
Pasta roller

5 large egg yolks
1 large egg
1 tsp extra virgin olive oil
2 cups all-purpose flour
1 tbsp water, as needed
Semolina rimacinata, for dusting

PASTA

Wrap the dough in plastic and rest it for at least 25 minutes, after which it should be smooth and tender enough to take an imprint when poked, but stiff enough that it takes a bit of force to press down. There shouldn't be any dry flour bits, but if there are, simply spritz the dough with a bit of water. Rest it, wrapped, for another 10 minutes before rolling.

Porcini Pasta Dough

Make the dough: Using the ingredients listed here, follow the instructions for the egg pasta dough on page 127. Make sure to let your dough rest for at least 30 minutes.

5 large egg yolks

3 large eggs

1 tbsp extra virgin olive oil

3 cups all-purpose flour

½ cup dried porcini, ground, or 3 tbsp porcini powder

Water, as needed

Rolling Pasta Dough

Portion the dough: To avoid the pasta sheets drying, it is best to go through the process of rolling, cutting and filling the pasta working with one-fifth of the dough at a time, and then repeat the process for each portion of the remaining dough. To begin, cut off about one-fifth of the dough [1]. Carefully wrap the rest so it doesn't dry out, and set aside.

Roll the dough: Set the pasta roller to the widest possible setting. Flatten the cut-off dough piece slightly with your hands or with a rolling pin to about ½ inch thick [2]. Carefully and slowly begin feeding your dough through the machine [3]. Roll it on the same setting again. Gradually reduce the settings by one notch, passing the pasta sheet through the rollers twice at each setting until it is about 8 inches long [4].

Fold the dough: Open the pasta roller back up to the widest setting and fold the dough onto itself like a letter [5, 6]. Rotate the dough 90 degrees and repeat the whole rolling process [7] until the pasta sheet is as thin as the recipe requires [8].

Cut and shape the pasta: Follow the instructions in the recipe to cut and shape your first sheet pasta, and set aside.

Repeat the process: Repeat the rolling process from the beginning, working with equal-sized chunks of the remaining dough.

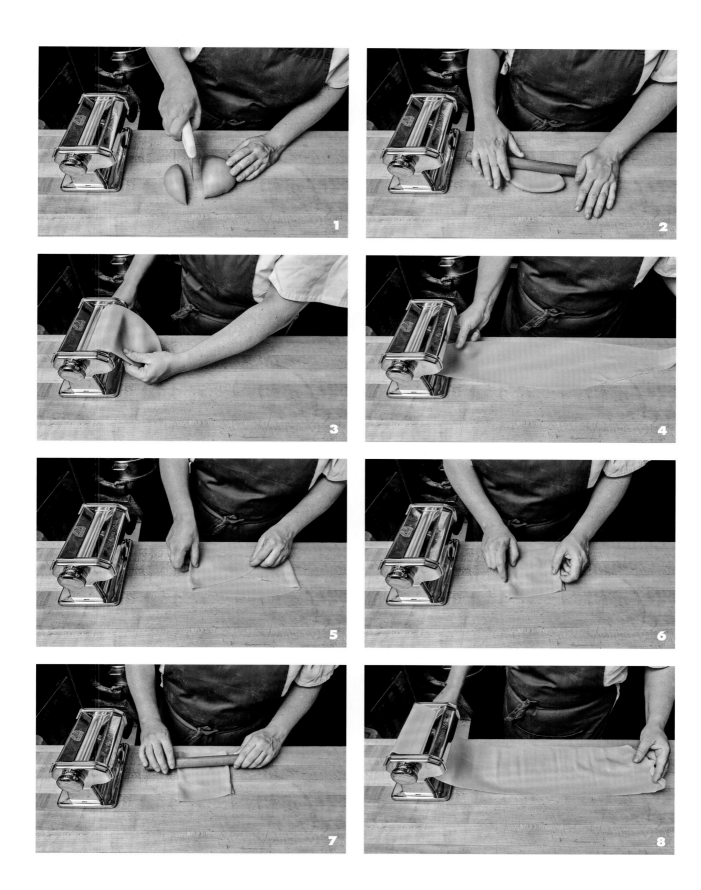

Strozzapreti alla Gricia with Artichokes

SERVES 6–8 **SUMMER**

This is our take on an off-menu pasta dish they make at Da Cesare, a restaurant in Rome that our friend Katie Parla introduced us to (thanks, Katie!). We add artichokes to ours and make it with strozzapreti because we love the shape and the many stories behind its name. According to one of them, strozzapreti (priest strangler in Italian) comes from an old Italian legend about a priest who choked on the pasta because it was so good that he tried to eat it too quickly. Very relatable if you ask us. Plus, we love the variety in texture you get from the twisted pasta, marinated artichokes and crispy bits of guanciale.

Make the dough: Mix and rest the semolina dough following the directions on p. 124.

Roll the dough: Working in batches, follow the pasta dough rolling instructions on p. 130 to make 1/16-inch-thick sheets (you should begin to see the wood grain of your table through it). Depending on your machine, this should be the second- or third-to-last setting.

Cut the dough: Lightly dust the first pasta sheet with semolina, and carefully fold it up into a flat roll. Cut the roll lengthwise into two pieces roughly 2½ inches wide. Unroll the sheets, cut them into 6- to 7-inch-long sheets, and stack them, dusting with more semolina as you go to make sure they don't stick together. Cut the sheets into ¾-inch strips. (Strozzapreti is an irregular pasta shape, so don't be too fussy—we love to celebrate imperfections over here.)

Shape the pasta: Shuffle the strips into a pile, and working one at a time, roll each one in your palms back and forth (pretend it's the middle of winter and you're trying to keep your hands warm). The strip should now look like a rolled-up towel. Place it on a baking sheet lightly dusted with semolina.

Repeat the rolling, cutting and shaping process with the rest of the dough, working one portion at a time. Let the pasta dry for at least 30 minutes and up to 1 hour, tossing every so often to prevent sticking.

(continued)

1 batch Semolina Pasta Dough (p. 124)

Semolina rimacinata, for dusting

Sauce

1 tsp extra virgin olive oil + more to finish

3½ oz (100 g) guanciale or pancetta, cut into lardons (about 1 cup)

3 cloves garlic, minced

½ cup water or stock (chicken, vegetable or parmesan on p. 275)

1½ cups Marinated Artichokes (p. 284, but use 1 tbsp vinegar instead of ¼ cup, and reserve ½ cup cooking liquid) or good-quality oil-packed artichokes

5 tbsp unsalted butter, room temperature, cut into 1-inch cubes

¾ cup grated pecorino

¾ cup grated parmesan + more to finish

Freshly ground black pepper

Kosher salt

Render the guanciale: In a cold, large frying pan (not a cast-iron), place 1 tsp olive oil and the cubed guanciale. (You want the guanciale to warm up at the same time as the pan to allow the fat to render without crisping first.) Cook over medium heat, stirring occasionally, until the guanciale has rendered its fat and has started to crisp up, about 5 minutes.

Cook the pasta and make the sauce: Bring a large pot of salted water to a boil. For this next step, it's important to have all your ingredients at the ready and that the pasta and the sauce be done at the same time. The sauce can sit for a few extra minutes while the pasta cooks, but you want to make sure it is hot when the pasta is ready. Add the garlic to the guanciale and cook until fragrant, about 1 minute. Add the water, the artichokes and their cooking liquid and bring to a simmer. Meanwhile, gently add the strozzapreti to the pot of boiling water and cook until al dente, about 2 minutes.

Once the pasta is cooked and still hot, strain and transfer to a large metal bowl. Add the sauce and butter cubes and toss several times until the butter is melted and the strozzapreti is well coated. Quickly add the freshly grated pecorino and parmesan and a few twists of pepper. Toss vigorously until the sauce starts to thicken and become creamy. Taste and adjust the seasoning with salt and pepper.

Serve: Divide into bowls and top with extra parmesan and a drizzle of olive oil.

Linguine Verde with Shrimp and Guanciale

SERVES 4–6   SPRING

This was on the menu when we first opened the restaurant and it remains one of Julio's (DJ, model, one of our OG servers and an all-around renaissance man) favorite pasta dishes. This recipe is not complicated, but because it comes with marinated shrimps and involves coloring pasta with spinach puree, it looks really impressive. It's a simple yet effective way to wow your loved ones without requiring too much effort on your part.

Marinate the shrimp: Preheat the oven to 400°F. If you're using frozen shrimps, place them in a colander and thaw by running cold water over them. Peel the shrimps, reserving the shells to make the shrimp stock. In a large bowl, combine the shrimps, garlic, olive oil and chili flakes, and toss to coat evenly. Cover and refrigerate for at least 1 hour and up to 1 day.

Toast the shrimp shells: Spread the reserved shrimp shells on a baking sheet and bake in the oven until dry and fragrant, about 20 minutes. Remove from the oven and set aside.

Make the shrimp stock: In a medium pot, melt the butter over medium heat. Add the garlic and fresh chili, and sauté until the garlic is very fragrant and is just starting to change color. Add the toasted shrimp shells and the onions and continue cooking for another 2 minutes. Add the water and kombu and bring to a low simmer. Cook for 30 minutes, turn off the heat and let the stock steep for another 20 minutes. Using a colander set over a bowl, strain the shrimp stock and set aside. Discard the shells and aromatics.

Make the dough: Mix and rest the green semolina dough following the directions on p. 125.

Roll the dough: Working in batches, follow the pasta dough rolling instructions on p. 130 to make ⅟₁₆-inch-thick sheets (you should begin to see the wood grain of your table through it). Depending on your machine, this should be the second- or third-to-last setting.

(continued)

Shrimp

1 lb (450 g) fresh or frozen shell-on shrimps

3 cloves garlic, minced

4 tbsp extra virgin olive oil

⅛ tsp dried chili flakes or powder

Shrimp stock

2 tbsp unsalted butter

3 cloves garlic

1 fresh red chili (we like long red, red hot or red jalapeno), cut in half

1 onion, sliced

4 cups water

1 (about 3 × 4-inch) piece kombu (optional)

Linguine

1 batch Green Semolina Pasta Dough (p. 125)

Semolina rimacinata, for dusting

1 tsp extra virgin olive oil

5.2 oz (150 g) guanciale, thinly sliced

2 tbsp + 4 tbsp unsalted butter, divided

½ tsp kosher salt

1 cup white wine

3 cups baby spinach or torn adult spinach

½ cup Toasted Breadcrumbs (p. 251)

Shape the pasta: Lightly dust your work surface with semolina. Cut your rolled dough into 14-inch-long sheets. Use your roller's linguine attachment to cut the sheets. If you don't have a linguine attachment, dust the sheets with semolina and stack them together. Carefully roll them up and cut them into ¼-inch-wide noodles. Dust the noodles with semolina as you go and lay them onto a baking sheet to dry for about 20–30 minutes, depending on the humidity level in your kitchen. (Throw a towel over them to slow down the drying if you need more time as they'll start breaking if they get too dry.) Form the linguine into a nest by wrapping a handful of noodles around your hand.

Repeat the rolling, cutting and shaping process with the rest of the dough, working one portion at a time. Store the linguine in an air-tight container in the fridge for up to 1 day or in the freezer for up to 3 months.

Cook the guanciale: In a large frying pan (not a cast-iron), add 1 tsp olive oil and the guanciale slices. Gently heat the pan over medium heat and cook, stirring occasionally, until the guanciale has rendered its fat and has started to crisp up. (Be patient and keep the heat low; this step can take a long time.) Once the guanciale is crispy, transfer the contents of the pan to a colander set over a heatproof bowl. Reserve 2 tbsp fat and set aside.

Cook the shrimp: Return the guanciale along with the reserved fat to the pan and turn up the heat to medium-high. Add 2 tbsp butter and cook until it starts to foam. Add the shrimp in an even layer, sprinkle with ½ tsp kosher salt and toss, until they are just cooked, 1–2 minutes. Transfer to a plate and set aside.

Make the sauce: Deglaze the pan with the white wine and cook until it is reduced by half. Add 2 cups shrimp stock and continue cooking until it is reduced by half.

Cook the linguine and assemble: Meanwhile, bring a large pot of salted water to a boil. Add the linguine and cook, stirring occasionally, for about 2 minutes. Drain the pasta and add to the sauce, along with the spinach and 4 tbsp butter. Cook, tossing often, until the pasta is well coated and the sauce has thickened, about 2 minutes. Toss the shrimp and guanciale back in. Taste and adjust the seasoning with salt.

Serve: Divide the pasta and top with toasted breadcrumbs.

Corn Agnolotti

SERVES 4   SUMMER

Corn in Quebec has a super-short and highly anticipated season. People love it so much here that they host these traditional parties called *épluchette de blé d'inde* (corn cob shucking) where guests are asked to shuck all the cobs and the person who finds the special cob (usually dyed red or blue) becomes the king or queen of the party. Because making agnolotti is already pretty labor-intensive, hosting a shucking party is a really fun way to trick your friends into doing all the prep for you, so we highly recommend it.

Cook the corn: Heat a medium saucepan on medium heat. Add the olive oil, butter, onions and garlic and cook until the onions start to sweat and become translucent, about 10 minutes. Add the corn and fresh chili and season with ½ tsp salt and the pepper. Turn the heat up to medium-high and cook until the corn smells sweet and the mixture begins to caramelize, 5–8 minutes.

Make the filling: Add the cream and reduce the heat to a simmer, cooking until the liquid is reduced by two-thirds, about 10 minutes. Remove from the heat and allow to cool slightly. Discard the fresh chili. Place the cooled mixture into a blender and add the ricotta and grated parmesan. Blend until smooth and homogeneous. Taste and adjust the seasoning with salt and pepper. Let the filling cool some more, then transfer to a piping bag and refrigerate until ready to use.

Make the dough: Follow the instructions for the egg pasta dough on p. 127.

Roll the dough: Working in batches, follow the pasta dough rolling instructions on p. 130 to make ¹⁄₁₆-inch-thick sheets (you should begin to see the wood grain of your table through it). Depending on your machine, this should be the second- or third-to-last setting.

(continued)

Special Equipment
Blender
Pasta roller
Piping bag

Corn Filling
4 tbsp extra virgin olive oil
2 tbsp unsalted butter
1 cup diced onions
1 clove garlic, minced
2 cups fresh corn kernels (about 2–3 ears of corn)
1 fresh chili (we like cayenne), cut in half
1 tsp kosher salt, divided
¼ tsp freshly ground black pepper
⅔ cup 35% cream
¾ cup Ricotta (p. 273 or store-bought)
1 cup grated parmesan

Agnolotti
1 batch Egg Pasta Dough (p. 127)
Semolina rimacinata, for dusting
½ cup unsalted butter, cut into ½-inch cubes, divided
1 cup fresh corn kernels
3 cloves garlic, minced
⅔ cup white wine
1 cup chicken stock or Parmesan Stock (p. 275)
15–20 saffron threads (optional)
Kosher salt and freshly ground black pepper

Serving
¼ cup minced fresh chives
6 tbsp crumbled goat cheese (optional)

Cut and fill the pasta: Lightly dust your work surface with semolina. Using a sharp knife, cut the dough widthwise into manageable 10-inch pieces, then cut those lengthwise into two 2½-inch-wide strips [1]. Unroll the first piece of dough and cover the other so it doesn't dry out. Following the length of the pasta strip, carefully pipe the corn filling along the center [2].

Shape the pasta: Lightly flour a baking sheet and set aside. Spritz the dough with some water, and beginning with the edge closest to you, fold the dough over the filling like a blanket [3]. Gently press the dough against the filling to eliminate air bubbles [4]. Fold the pasta over the filled section once more away from yourself [5]. (It should now look like a long tube of filled pasta.) Starting from the left, pinch down the dough with your fingers at 3-inch intervals to create little agnolotti pockets [6]. Using a rolling cutter or a knife, cut each agnolotti along the pinched seams [7]. Transfer to the floured baking sheet [8].

Repeat the rolling, cutting and shaping process with the rest of the dough, working one portion at a time. Cover the agnolotti loosely with a kitchen towel until ready to cook, or freeze them in one layer and transfer them to a container as soon as they are solid to prevent cracking. They will keep in the freezer for up to 1 month.

Make the sauce: Bring a large pot of salted water to a boil. Meanwhile, in a medium pot, heat one-third of the butter cubes on medium heat. Add the corn kernels and minced garlic and cook for 2 minutes, reducing the heat to avoid coloring. Deglaze the pan with the white wine and reduce until almost dry. Add the chicken stock and saffron threads and bring to a simmer.

Cook the agnolotti and assemble: While the sauce is simmering and reducing, add the agnolotti to the pot of boiling water and cook, stirring occasionally, for 3 minutes. Drain the pasta and add to the sauce, bottom facing down. (This part of the pasta is a bit thicker and can benefit from more cooking time.) Add the remaining butter cubes and swirl the pan gently until the sauce is smooth and has thickened, 2–3 minutes. Taste and adjust the seasoning with salt and pepper.

Serve: Divide the pasta onto plates and garnish with chopped chives and crumbled goat cheese.

Raviolo Giardino

SERVES 4 (2 RAVIOLO PER PERSON)   **SUMMER**

This flower-laced raviolo is a timebomb in pasta form. If you don't do it right, it will explode in the water. Roll the dough too thin and the herbs will poke holes. Roll it too thick and you won't even see the flowers. It's a difficult recipe that, when done right, yields striking results. It's a beautiful way to showcase everything that blooms in the summer. In the winter, you can make it with cold-weather herbs like sage and rosemary.

Make the ricotta filling: In a food processor, place the ricotta, parsley, chopped ricotta salata, chives, olive oil, lemon juice, salt and pepper. Blend until smooth, then transfer to a piping bag and refrigerate until ready to use.

Make the dough: Follow the instructions for the egg pasta dough on p. 127.

Roll the top pasta sheet with herbs and flowers: Cutting one-sixth of the dough (instead of one-fifth) and working in batches, follow the pasta dough rolling instructions on p. 130 to make 1/16-inch-thick sheets (you should begin to see the wood grain of your table through it). Spritz with a bit of water to moisten the pasta sheet slightly. Scatter flower petals and finely picked leaves on the surface of the pasta sheet [1]. Carefully lay a second sheet of pasta (rolled to the same thickness) on top of the first sheet [2]. Using a rolling pin, gently roll over both sheets to seal. Open your pasta machine to a slightly larger setting than what was just used to roll the sheets. Slowly roll the flower sheet through the machine until you achieve a 1/16-inch-thick sheet [3]. Fold gently and set aside in a plastic bag or sealed container to prevent drying. If your dough is sticking to itself, dust very lightly with flour. If it is getting dry, spritz lightly with water.

Roll the bottom pasta sheet: In a small bowl, lightly beat one egg with a fork. Roll out another 1/16-inch-thick sheet of pasta. Brush it lightly with the beaten egg. Using a 6-inch ring mold, press gently to mark circles spaced 1 inch apart.

(continued)

Special Equipment
Food processor
Piping bag
Pasta roller
6-inch ring mold

Ricotta filling
1 cup Ricotta (p. 273)
½ cup chopped fresh parsley
¼ cup finely chopped ricotta salata
¼ cup chopped fresh chives
¼ cup extra virgin olive oil
½ tbsp fresh lemon juice
½ tsp kosher salt
¼ tsp freshly ground black pepper

Raviolo
1 batch Egg Pasta Dough (p. 127)
1 cup fresh herbs and edible flowers (chervil, fennel fronds, pansies, borage, nasturtium, anise hyssop, etc.)
Semolina rimacinata, for dusting
1 large egg
8 large egg yolks
Flaky sea salt
6 tbsp unsalted butter, divided
Handful fresh herbs (verbena, sage or thyme leaves)
2 cups chicken stock or Parmesan Stock (p. 275)

Serving

1 handful freshly picked herbs and flowers (chervil, fennel fronds, pansies, borage, nasturtium, anise hyssop, basil, lemon verbena, mint, chives)

½ cup hazelnuts, toasted (see p. 253)

Flaky sea salt

Stuff the raviolo: Using the filled piping bag, create a small ring of ricotta filling inside the marked circles [4]. (You should leave about ½ inch on the outer edge, and each inner ring should be big enough to fit one egg yolk). Using a spoon, gently place one egg yolk in the center of each ricotta filling ring (if one breaks, don't use it). The egg yolks should not sit any higher than the surface of the ricotta to avoid breaking once the top layer of pasta is added. Sprinkle each yolk with a pinch of flaky sea salt.

Close the raviolo: Very carefully, drape the flower pasta sheet on top of the ricotta and egg mounds [5]. Make sure to allow for plenty of extra pasta sheet to fully cover the ricotta and egg mounds. Using the same ring mold, cut out around each raviolo and remove the excess dough [6]. Working one at a time, seal the raviolo by pinching lightly, creating small folds that curl up (this shape will help hold the sauce in the plate). Store the finished raviolo in a closed but not airtight container lined with semolina for no more than 1 day.

Make the sauce: Bring a wide pot of salted water to a boil. Meanwhile, in a wide pan, add 4 tbsp butter and fresh herbs. Cook on medium-low, swishing the pan around to ensure even cooking, and allow the butter to brown but not burn, about 4 minutes. Turn the heat down to low and add the chicken stock to stop the butter from cooking further.

Cook the raviolo and assemble: Using a spatula, very carefully add four raviolo at a time (you might have to put fewer at a time, depending on the size of your pot) to the pot of boiling water. Cook for 3 minutes. Using a slotted spoon or a small strainer, transfer the raviolo to the sauce. Reduce the sauce, add 2 tbsp butter and gently toss the raviolo in the sauce to coat, about 1 minute. If you'd like your egg to be runny, make sure not to cook the raviolo in the butter for too long. Cook the remaining raviolo and toss in the sauce.

Serve: Place two raviolos per plate and top with drippings of sauce. Garnish with fresh herbs and flowers, toasted hazelnuts and flaky sea salt.

GETTING SOBER MADE ME FALL BACK IN LOVE WITH WINE

By Ryan Gray

My coming of age as a sommelier came around the time when chefs started to really carve their way into mainstream culture, thanks in part to series like Anthony Bourdain's *No Reservations* and Vice's *Chef's Night Out*. I really admired the people I saw on those shows. They had big personalities, huge appetites and an even bigger hunger for partying.

Our industry was having a moment because, as restaurant professionals, we knew how to make excess look like a good time, even when it wasn't. During those years, being the person who could outdrink everyone wasn't just cool, it was something you wore like a badge of honor. The expression we used at Joe Beef and Liverpool House, where I worked, was "kill them"—hospitality wasn't about giving people a pleasant dining experience, it was about who could drink the most Burgundy wine and do the most shots.

Until I got sober a few years into opening my first restaurant, Nora Gray, I never understood being a sommelier as something that was separate from getting wasted all the time. Daytime tastings with winemakers would turn into boozy lunches, and next thing I knew, I'd be at the restaurant opening bottles and putting on a show for people. Someone's in from out of town? We need to make sure we stay relevant by raiding the wine cellar at 3 a.m. and pulling bottles so rare most people can't find them anywhere. Doing that kind of stuff made me feel like I was one of the big guys. But when my addiction took over, I felt like I was just going through the motions—like a sad clown who forgot why he even started working at the circus in the first place.

I celebrated my 33rd birthday in rehab, where I began to untangle the addiction from my profession. I'll admit that my experience with sobriety is not like most people's (everyone's is different, really), although it is not completely singular. When I got out, I continued to manage the wine program while working service at Nora Gray. I had to constantly turn down glasses offered by well-meaning guests, telling them that I no longer drank. It stumped a few people at first because they knew me as "that guy," the one they had seen stumbling drunk and breaking a phone on an old episode of *Munchies*.

The first time I tasted wine again was eight months after I got sober. I was in post-recovery therapy. I had a really strong program but still wasn't sure wine would ever touch my lips again. We were hosting a Nora Gray event in Toronto—a six-course tasting menu with wine pairings that guests had spent a lot of money to attend. I had selected all the wines beforehand, all bottles I was quite familiar with, when one appeared to be off. With no one else able to confirm my suspicion, I took a deep breath and took a sip. I swished it around in my mouth and drew a little air in like I had a million times before. Then I spat it out. It was a true aha moment for me. I didn't turn around to finish the bottle. I didn't want to. I didn't need to. This was what it meant to be a wine professional. After that night, I slowly began to taste wine professionally again. To this day, I still haven't swallowed a drop.

From that moment on, the way I related to my job completely shifted. I became more passionate about wine than I'd ever been before. By not drinking, I allowed myself to fall in love with everything I found truly interesting about it (especially the winemakers and their stories), as opposed to focusing so much on the partying aspect of the industry.

Whereas my definition of hospitality before was linked to excess and satisfying my own ego, now I take actual pleasure in connecting and sharing with people on a deeper level.

I don't feel the need to perform or please anyone anymore. People that come into my restaurants have an amazing experience because we created a healthy environment in which we can give proper hospitality that's aimed at making people feel good in the moment, as well as the next day when they wake up.

People often ask me if I "miss it." I don't. The irony is that I began to experience the best parts of this métier only after getting sober. Getting to travel to vineyards across Italy, making lifelong friendships with winemakers and building businesses that are both successful and healthy places for the people who work in them: there is nothing to miss, especially not the hangover.

Spaghetti Ubriachi

SERVES 4–6 AUTUMN

When Ryan stopped drinking, Janice had to find a way for him to eat wine instead of chugging it. That's how this recipe was born. Just kidding—this is just a really great dish we love to make around harvest time in Quebec, when the weather is starting to turn a little colder. We like to make a very large batch and eat from a single giant bowl with all of our closest friends (think *Lady and the Tramp*, but platonic). If you don't feel like making your own pasta dough, this recipe is still delicious with store-bought spaghetti. As for the wine, just make sure you use a dry red you actually like, since its flavor is going to infuse everything from the dough to the sauce.

Reduce the wine: In a medium pot over medium-high heat, add the wine and bring to a boil. Cook, uncovered, until the wine has reduced by two-thirds, 20–25 minutes. Let it cool completely. Set ½ cup aside for the pasta dough (p. 126) and reserve the rest (about 1 cup) for the sauce. This step can be done ahead of time.

Make the dough: Follow the instructions for the red wine semolina pasta dough on p. 126.

Roll the dough: Working in batches, follow the pasta dough rolling instructions on p. 130 to make ⅛-inch-thick sheets.

Shape the pasta: Lightly dust your work surface. Cut your rolled dough into 14-inch-long sheets. Use your roller's spaghetti attachment to cut the sheets, then dust the cut noodles with semolina as you go and lay them carefully onto a baking sheet. Let dry for about 20–30 minutes (depending on the humidity level in your kitchen), tossing them gently with the semolina every 10 minutes or so to make sure they're not sticking together or drying up. While the noodles are still malleable, form them into a nest by wrapping a handful of spaghetti around your hand.

(continued)

Special Equipment
Pasta roller with a spaghetti attachment

Red Wine Spaghetti
1 bottle red wine
1 batch Red Wine Semolina Pasta Dough (p. 126)
Semolina rimacinata, for dusting

Wine Sauce
1½ tbsp extra virgin olive oil + more to finish
6 cloves garlic, finely chopped
½ tsp dried chili flakes
8 tbsp unsalted butter, cut into 1-inch pieces, divided
Kosher salt

Serving
Extra virgin olive oil
Parmesan, finely grated

Repeat the rolling, cutting and shaping process with the rest of the dough, working one portion at a time. Store in an airtight container for up to 1 day in the fridge or for up to 3 months in the freezer.

Make the red wine sauce: Bring a large pot of salted water to a boil. Meanwhile, in a separate large pot, heat the olive oil over medium heat. Add the garlic, chili flakes and 1 tbsp butter. Cook, stirring occasionally, until the garlic is very fragrant but not browned, about 3 minutes. Add the reserved reduced wine, cover and lower the heat down to a minimum while you cook the pasta.

Cook the spaghetti and assemble: Add the spaghetti to the pot of boiling water and cook, stirring occasionally, about 2 minutes. If using store-bought pasta, cook it until very al dente, 2 minutes shy of the recommended cooking time. Drain the pasta and add to the sauce, along with the remaining 7 tbsp butter. Turn the heat up to medium and bring the sauce to a simmer. Cook, tossing often, until the pasta is well coated and the sauce has thickened, about 3 minutes. Taste and season with salt if needed.

Serve: Divide the pasta among bowls or put on a giant platter for a family-style meal. Drizzle with olive oil and top with lots of grated parmesan.

Suppli al Telefono

MAKES 15–20 SUPPLI   ALL SEASONS

Suppli are a classic Roman street food that you'll also find served in pizzerias like Bonci, in Rome. They're essentially little rice or pasta balls with stringy mozzarella cheese tucked in the middle, which when melted and pulled apart, looks like one of those tin can telephone strings we made as kids. This is our basic suppli recipe, but you can easily choose your own adventure and substitute the aromatics in the risotto, or even swap the rice for polenta or spaghetti.

Cook the risotto: The risotto should be made a few hours or even a day ahead since the rice needs to cool down completely before shaping the balls. In a small pot over medium heat, bring the stock to a simmer. Turn off the heat and set aside. In a deep skillet or a shallow pot with a heavy bottom, heat the olive oil on medium heat. Add the onions and garlic and cook until translucent but not browned at all, 5–8 minutes. Add the rice and bay leaf and season with salt and pepper. Toast, stirring frequently to prevent burning, until the rice becomes glossy, about 5 minutes. Add the white wine and cook until completely absorbed, 1–2 minutes.

Start adding some warm stock, about ¼ cup at a time, just enough so that it covers the rice. Stir once after ladling the stock to prevent sticking, but not more than that (stirring constantly will push the flavors to develop too much). Adjust the heat if you notice that the liquid is boiling too hard or getting absorbed too quickly. When most of the stock has reduced, add another ¼ cup. Continue this process until all the stock has been added and the rice is tender—but not mushy—16–20 minutes. If the rice still feels too crunchy after that, simply add more water and continue cooking until it's ready.

Add the tomato sauce and stir until heated through. Remove from the heat and fold in the grated parmesan. Taste and adjust with salt and pepper. Spread the risotto on a baking sheet in a ½-inch layer and transfer to the fridge until cooled down completely.

(continued)

Special Equipment
Frying thermometer

Risotto
2 cups low-sodium chicken stock or Parmesan Stock (p. 275)

1 tbsp extra virgin olive oil

1 small onion, diced

1 clove garlic, minced

½ cup carnaroli or arborio rice

1 bay leaf

1 tsp kosher salt, to taste

Freshly ground black pepper

2 tbsp white wine

½ cup Tomato Sauce (p. 255)

½ cup grated parmesan

Suppli
5.2 oz (150 g) low-moisture mozzarella, cut into ¼ × 1-inch sticks

½ cup all-purpose flour

5 large eggs or 1 cup egg whites

2 cups unseasoned Toasted Breadcrumbs (follow the instructions on p. 251, but omit the seasoning)

Vegetable oil, enough for frying

Kosher salt

1 cup Tomato Sauce (p. 255), for dipping

Shape the balls: Use an ice-cream scoop or a large spoon to divide the risotto into 15–20 golf-ball-size balls. Using your hands (wet them beforehand to prevent sticking), press one cheese stick into the center of each ball. Seal the hole with rice and roll the ball between your palms into the shape of a football, making sure the cheese is completely covered. Set on a baking sheet and repeat with the remaining balls. Chill them in the freezer until firm, at least 1 hour and up to 2 days.

Prepare the breading ingredients: Prepare three small bowls. Put the flour in the first bowl. In the second bowl, thin out the eggs by whisking in a few tablespoons of water as necessary. In the third bowl, put the unseasoned breadcrumbs.

Bread the balls: Drop a ball in the flour and shake off the excess. Dip it into the egg mixture and let the excess drip off. Next, roll it in the breadcrumb bowl, pressing the crumbs firmly into the suppli, and put on a baking sheet. Repeat with the remaining balls until they are all breaded. The breaded suppli will keep in the fridge for 1 day before frying or up to 1 month in the freezer. Thaw the suppli, uncovered, for 1 hour before frying.

Preheat the oven and heat the oil: Preheat the oven to 400°F and place a rack in the middle. Pour 2 inches of vegetable oil into a medium pot. Attach a frying thermometer to the side of the pot and heat the oil to 325°F–350°F.

Fry and bake the suppli: Working in small batches, fry each suppli until golden brown, about 2 minutes. Using a slotted spoon, transfer each suppli to a baking sheet and season lightly with salt. Once all the suppli are on the baking sheet, transfer to the oven and bake until they are heated through and the cheese has melted, 5–8 minutes. Serve right away with a side of tomato sauce for dipping.

Saffron Bucatini with Clams and Bottarga

SERVES 4–6 **WINTER**

Readers, if he:
· Is long and thick
· Leaves you satisfied
· Comes with saffron, clams and bottarga
He's not your man. He's this bucatini recipe. Better put a ring on it.

Purge the clams: Some shops will sell pre-purged clams, but it's never a bad idea to give them an extra rinse. In a very large bowl, add the water, salt and clams. Let them sit until the sand has purged, changing the water every 30 minutes, for a total of 1–2 hours depending on the amount of sand. Using your hands or a slotted spoon to avoid transferring any of the purged sand, carefully transfer the clams to a colander. Discard the water. Throw out the clams that are already open. Cover the rest with a damp towel and keep cold.

Make the sauce: Bring a large pot of salted water to a boil. Meanwhile, in a small bowl, add the white wine and saffron, and set aside. In a separate large pot, add the drained clams, 1/3 cup butter, olive oil, minced garlic and chili flakes. Cook on medium-high heat until the butter has melted and the garlic is fragrant, 3 minutes. Add the wine and saffron, cover and bring back to a boil, cooking until the clams begin to open, about 5 minutes once the wine mixture is boiling. (The clams are cooked when they open, and some will open sooner than others, so keep checking.) Turn off the heat, transfer the clams to a bowl and cover to keep warm.

Cook the bucatini and assemble: Add the bucatini to the pot of boiling water and cook, stirring occasionally, until very al dente, 2 minutes shy of the recommended cooking time. Drain the pasta and add it to the sauce along with the remaining 1/3 cup butter and the spinach. Turn the heat up to medium-high and toss until the pasta is well coated and the sauce is creamy and has thickened, about 1–2 minutes. Add the clams back into the pot and toss. Taste and adjust the seasoning with salt.

Serve: Divide into bowls and serve with a drizzle of chili oil and shaved bottarga.

Clams

20 cups water

1/2 cup kosher salt

3 lb (1.4 kg) clams (we like littleneck, cherrystone or steamer clams)

Bucatini

2 cups white wine

1/2 tsp saffron

2/3 cup unsalted butter, divided

3 tbsp extra virgin olive oil

5 cloves garlic, minced

1/2 tsp dried chili flakes

1 lb (450 g) bucatini (store-bought or make plain linguine following instructions on p. 135)

4 cups spinach

Kosher salt

Chris's Crispy Chili Oil (optional, p. 256)

Bottarga (optional)

Farfalle with Fava Beans and Morels

SERVES 4–6 SPRING

We're officially starting a campaign so that people stop calling farfalle "bowtie pasta." Not only does it not mean bowtie in Italian (farfalle means butterflies) but calling it that is doing this pasta shape a disservice. Butterflies are awesome—they can fly, they represent rebirth and transformation and they're colorful and beautiful. Bowties, on the other hand, well . . . you know . . . they're kind of a thing. Anyway, this is a wonderful pasta dish in which the quintessential springtime bean, the fava, symbolizes nature's comeback and ground porcini mushrooms impart both color and texture to the wings of our butterfly pasta.

Make the dough: Follow the instructions for the porcini pasta dough on p. 129.

Roll the dough: Working in batches, follow the pasta dough rolling instructions on p. 130 to make ⅛-inch-thick sheets.

Shape the pasta: Lightly dust a baking sheet with semolina. Using a pasta cutter and working with one sheet at a time, keeping the rest of the dough covered, cut each sheet of pasta lengthwise into three 2½-inch-long strips, then cut again crosswise every 3 inches to create 2½ × 3-inch dough rectangles. (Use a zigzag cutter for the crosswise cuts to give your farfalle ruffled edges.) Once all your rectangles are cut, discard the trimmed dough and begin to shape each rectangle into little bows.

Gather each piece at the center with a series of little folds on the long side (the ruffled edges should be on the outside of the bow), making sure to pinch down the center so that the dough is not too thick. Place the farfalle on the floured baking sheet and set aside, uncovered, for at least 30 minutes or until you are ready to cook them.

(continued)

1 batch Porcini Pasta Dough (p. 129)

Semolina rimacinata, for dusting

Morel Cream Sauce

2 cups white wine

3 shallots, thinly sliced

2 cups 35% cream

2 cups dried morels, divided

2 tsp kosher salt

Beans + Assembly

3 lb (1.4 kg) fava beans, peeled (about 2 cups shelled)

½ tsp freshly ground black pepper + more to finish

1 cup chicken stock or Parmesan Stock (p. 275)

½ cup unsalted butter

2 cups grated parmesan + more to finish

1 cup grated pecorino

Kosher salt

Extra virgin olive oil, to finish

Repeat the rolling, cutting and shaping process with the rest of the dough, working one portion at a time. If you aren't ready to cook them just yet, cover the farfalle loosely with a kitchen towel or freeze them in one layer and transfer them to a container as soon as they are solid to prevent cracking. They will keep in the freezer for up to 3 months.

Make the sauce and rehydrate the morels: In a medium pot over medium-high heat, combine the wine and the shallots. Bring to a simmer and continue cooking, uncovered, until the wine has reduced by two-thirds, about 20–25 minutes. Turn the heat down to low and add the cream and ½ cup dried morels. Cook for 20 minutes, then turn off the heat. Cover the pot and let the mushrooms steep in the sauce for 40 minutes. Meanwhile, place the remaining dried morels in a heatproof bowl. Bring a small pot of water to a boil and pour enough hot water over the morels to cover them entirely. Let them steep until you're ready to finish the sauce.

Strain the sauce, pressing on the morels and shallots to extract any remaining liquid. Discard the morels and shallots. Return the sauce to the pot, strain the rehydrated morels you have steeping in the other pot, add them to the sauce and bring to a low simmer. Cook for 5 minutes, taste and add 2 tsp salt. Remove from the heat and let cool.

Blanch the fava beans: Prepare a bowl of ice water. Bring a medium pot of salted water to a boil. Add the beans and blanch until tender but not mushy, about 2 minutes. Transfer the fava beans to the ice bath to stop them from cooking any further. Drain.

Cook the pasta and assemble: Bring a large pot of salted water to a boil. In a large pan over medium heat, toast the freshly ground black pepper until fragrant, 30 seconds. Add the morel cream sauce, chicken stock and blanched fava beans. Bring to a simmer. Meanwhile, add the farfalle to the pot of boiling water, stirring occasionally, about 2 minutes. Drain the pasta and add to the sauce, along with the butter. Cook and toss until the pasta is well coated and the sauce has slightly thickened, about 1 minute. Turn off the heat and add the parmesan and pecorino, tossing vigorously until the sauce starts to thicken and become creamy. Taste and adjust the seasoning with salt and pepper.

Serve: Divide into bowls and top with extra parmesan and a drizzle of olive oil.

Koginut Squash and Sage Caramelle

SERVES 4–6 **AUTUMN**

Caramelle is a really good contender for the cutest pasta shape of all time. It's essentially a candy wrapper made of egg pasta dough and, in this case, filled with our favorite squash (find more ways to use koginut squash on p. 97). Don't fret if you can't find koginut squash at the market (it's not that common). Just swap it for varieties that are somewhere on the sweeter side of the squash spectrum—think candy—like kabocha, buttercup or red kuri squash.

Cook the espresso butter a day ahead (optional): In a small pot, bring the butter and ground coffee to a low simmer over medium heat. Remove from the heat, cover and let it rest overnight at room temperature. The following day, gently reheat the butter over medium heat to loosen. Use a coffee filter to strain the espresso butter, then set aside.

Poach and roast the squash: Preheat the oven to 350°F. In a medium pot, combine the squash wedges, milk, sage leaves, nutmeg, salt and pepper and bring to a low simmer over medium heat. Cook gently until the squash is fork-tender, about 20 minutes. Using a slotted spoon or a small strainer, transfer the squash pieces and the sage leaves onto a baking sheet and spread evenly. Reserve the leftover milk to make the ricotta. Bake the squash in the oven to allow some of the excess moisture to evaporate, about 10 minutes.

Make the ricotta: While the squash is drying out, use the reserved milk and the lemon juice to make the ricotta following the instructions on p. 273. Note that this step takes at least 1 hour from start to finish.

Prepare the filling: In a blender or food processor, combine the squash and ricotta and pulse until smooth. Taste and adjust the seasoning with salt and pepper. Transfer the filling to a piping bag.

Make the dough: Follow the instructions for the egg pasta dough on p. 127.

Special Equipment
Instant-read thermometer
Blender or food processor
Pastry bag
Pasta roller

Espresso Butter (optional)
1 cup unsalted butter, cold, cut into cubes
½ cup ground coffee

Squash Filling
½ small koginut squash (10½ oz/300 g), peeled, seeded and cut into wedges
2 cups whole milk
A few leaves fresh sage
⅛ whole nutmeg, grated, or ⅛ tsp ground nutmeg
Kosher salt and freshly ground black pepper
3–5 tbsp fresh lemon juice

Caramelle
1 batch Egg Pasta Dough (p. 127)
¼ cup unsalted butter, cold, cut into cubes
A small handful fresh sage leaves
½ cup chicken or vegetable stock or Parmesan Stock (p. 275)
Kosher salt and freshly ground black pepper

(continued)

Roll the dough: Working in batches, follow the pasta dough rolling instructions on p. 130 to make ⅛-inch-thick sheets.

Cut the dough sheet in rectangles (roughly 2½ × 4 inches). If you notice the dough is drying out, spritz it with a bit of water.

Fill and shape the caramelle: Lightly flour a baking sheet and set aside. Grab your piping bag and pipe 2 tsp filling in the center of each rectangle. Spritz with water. Beginning with the edge closest to you (it should be the long side), fold the dough just over the filling, then fold it once more. Pinch the dough on both sides of the filled pocket to seal and create a candy wrapper shape. Place the caramelle on the floured baking sheet and cover loosely with a kitchen towel until ready to cook, or freeze them in one layer and transfer them to a container as soon as they are solid to prevent cracking.

Repeat the rolling, filling and shaping process with the rest of the dough. The caramelle will keep in the freezer for up to 1 month.

Cook the pasta and prepare the sauce: Bring a large pot of salted water to a boil. Meanwhile, in a large skillet, cook the butter cubes and sage leaves over medium-high heat. As the butter melts, swish the pan around and scatter the leaves to ensure even cooking. Allow the butter to brown, but not burn, and the leaves to get crispy, about 4 minutes. When the sage leaves are nice and crispy, set them aside for garnish. Pour in the stock and turn the heat down to low. Gently add the caramelle to the pot of boiling water and cook until al dente, about 2–3 minutes. Strain and add them to the skillet and toss to emulsify the pasta and sauce together. Taste and do a final seasoning adjustment if necessary.

Serve: Divide the pasta into bowls and garnish with crispy sage leaves and a drizzle of espresso butter (optional). Serve immediately.

Tagliatelle with Rosemary Sugo

SERVES 4   WINTER

A version of this recipe has been on the menu since day one, and some of the staff (hi, Ellen!) have even threatened to push us down the stairs if we take it off. That is how strongly people feel when you try to take away the most comforting dish they've ever had. The ragu is technically a Sunday sauce (a traditional Italian pasta sauce made with all the odd bits of meat you have left at the end of the week). For ours, we braise beef short ribs and pork baby back ribs together with tomatoes, wine and lots of rosemary.

Salt the ribs the night before (optional): Place the ribs in a large dish or bowl and sprinkle generously with kosher salt all over. Cover the ribs and store in the fridge overnight. The following day, uncover the ribs and pat dry.

Sear the ribs: Preheat the oven to 450°F. Lightly grease a large baking sheet with olive oil and line up the ribs on the tray so the meat of the pork ribs and the fat cap of the beef ribs are facing up. Roast the meat for 10–15 minutes until some color develops. Rotate and flip the pieces and continue to oven-sear for a further 10–15 minutes. Remove and let cool slightly.

Make the base: In a Dutch oven or ovenproof pot with a fitted lid, warm the olive oil over medium heat, then stir in the celery, carrots, onions and garlic cloves. Cook, stirring occasionally, until just starting to brown. Add the tomato paste and stir to combine, cooking a further 2 minutes. Add the rosemary sprig, bay leaf, canned tomatoes, white wine and chicken stock and bring to a boil. Once the sugo base has come to a boil, remove from the heat.

Braise the meat: Lower the oven temperature to 275°F. Add the seared ribs to the pot and cover with a lid. Transfer the pot to the oven and cook for 2 hours.

Make the dough: While the meat is braising, follow the instructions for the egg pasta dough on page 127.

(continued)

Special Equipment
Food mill or immersion blender

Sugo
1 rack pork baby back ribs, cut into 3 pieces
1 beef short rib
Kosher salt
⅓ cup extra virgin olive oil (or enough to coat the pan)
1 stalk celery, diced
1 large carrot, diced
1 medium onion, diced
½ head garlic, cloves separated
¼ cup tomato paste
1 sprig fresh rosemary
1 bay leaf
1 (28 oz/796 ml) can peeled whole tomatoes
½ cup white wine
2 cups low-sodium chicken stock

Assembly
1 batch Egg Pasta Dough (p. 127)
Semolina rimacinata, for dusting
1½ tbsp unsalted butter
Kosher salt and freshly ground black pepper
Extra virgin olive oil, to finish
Parmesan, finely grated
Fried sprig fresh rosemary (optional)

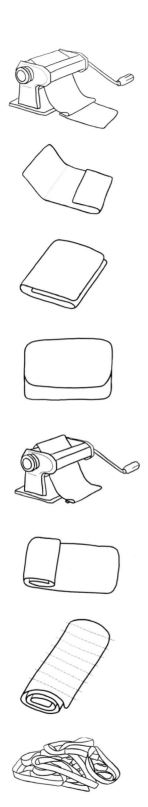

Roll out the pasta dough: Working in batches, follow the pasta dough rolling instructions on p. 130 to make ⅛-inch-thick sheets.

Cut and dry the noodles: Lightly flour a baking sheet and set aside. Cut the pasta sheets to about 14 inches in length. Dust the sheets with semolina and stack them together. Carefully roll them up and cut them into ⅓-inch-wide noodles. Grab a handful of noodles and shake them out so they don't stick together. Arrange the noodles on the floured baking sheet and let them dry, tossing every so often, until they feel a bit lighter and stiffer but not brittle.

Repeat the rolling, cutting and drying process with the remaining dough. The drying process can take up to 1 hour, depending on the ambient humidity of your kitchen.

Remove the meat from the oven: After 2 hours in the oven, check the meat for tenderness: it should separate easily without falling apart. (You may need to cook for up to 1 more hour to achieve this.) Remove the pot from the oven and allow the meat to cool down for at least 30 minutes in the cooking liquid.

Make the sugo: Once the braise is cool enough to handle, remove and discard (or compost) the bones, bay leaf and rosemary stems, then pick the meat off the bones and place in a separate bowl to cool further. Puree the remaining vegetables and tomato sauce/liquid by passing through a food mill or using an immersion blender for a few seconds until you have a nice but not too smooth sauce (keep it rustic!). Return the blended sauce to the pot and add the meat, shredding it into smaller pieces with your hands, then stir to combine.

Cook the tagliatelle and assemble: Bring a large pot of salted water to a boil. Cook the fresh tagliatelle until al dente, 2–3 minutes. Strain and return to the pot. Add the sugo and butter and stir to coat the pasta. Taste and adjust the seasoning with salt and pepper.

Serve: Divide the pasta among bowls. Add a drizzle of olive oil and lots of grated parmesan. Top with fried rosemary for some extra crunch.

Pacina Pici

SERVES 4   ALL SEASONS

When people say, "Picture your happy place," for us that's Pacina (more on that on p. 117). Whenever we travel to Italy to visit the winery, we like to cook these huge meals with the whole family. This is a dish Janice made there in early 2020 using hyper-local ingredients, like onions pulled fresh out of the ground in the rows of vines and a beautiful piece of coppa from the butcher in the village down the road.

Make the dough: Follow the instructions for the flour and semolina pasta dough on p. 126.

Roll and shape the pasta: Line a baking sheet with a kitchen towel and set aside. Unwrap the dough and flatten into a ½-inch-thick oval disk (it should be about 6 × 12 inches wide). Cut the disk lengthwise into two pieces roughly 6 inches long, then cut them into ⅓-inch-wide strips. Working one strip at a time on a lightly floured surface, leaving the rest of the dough covered to avoid drying, roll out each strip into a 6- to 8-inch-long pasta snake no thicker than a pencil. (Don't stress if your noodles aren't even or if some of them break while you're rolling—everyone knows no two snakes are alike. Or was it snowflakes? In all seriousness, pici is way more fun to eat the less perfect it is, so just have fun with it.) Place each pici on the lined baking sheet and lightly dust with semolina, and set aside, uncovered, for at least 10 minutes or until you are ready to cook them.

Make the sauce: Bring a large pot of salted water to a boil. In a separate large pot, heat the olive oil over medium-low heat. Add the coppa and cook gently, tossing occasionally, until just beginning to crisp, about 20 minutes. Add the garlic, pepper and chili flakes and cook until fragrant, 1 minute. Pour in the wine and tomato puree and continue cooking while you boil the pasta, about 5 minutes.

(continued)

Pici
1 batch Flour and Semolina Pasta Dough (p. 126)
Semolina rimacinata, for dusting

Sauce
½ cup extra virgin olive oil
1 cup cubed coppa or cured culatello
5 cloves garlic, finely chopped
1 tbsp freshly ground black pepper
½ tbsp dried chili flakes
½ cup white wine
1 (14 oz/398 ml) can tomato puree (1¾ cups)

Serving
Pecorino, finely grated
Extra virgin olive oil (preferably from Pacina)

Cook the pasta and assemble: Add the pici to the pot of boiling water and cook, stirring occasionally, until the noodles start to become tender, about 5 minutes. Drain the pasta, reserving ½ cup pasta water. Add the cooked pici and pasta water to the sauce and cook, tossing often, until the sauce has thickened a bit and begins to cling to the noodles.

Serve: Divide the pasta onto plates and serve immediately, topped with freshly grated pecorino and a drizzle of olive oil (preferably from Pacina).

MEAT + FISH

We've never had a lot of meat and fish mains on the menu at Elena, but these are the kinds of dishes that usually take center stage at our dinner parties. Whether we are cozying up over a long weekend up north where a porchetta seems like the only answer to our winter blues, or grilling chicken at Marley's mom's lake house after swimming around the tiny island all day, these are the dishes we want to make with our friends and family over and over again.

This chapter features a variety of seafoods and meats so that the next time you're at your local butcher shop or fishmonger, you can choose your own adventure and let whatever ingredient speaks to you most lead the way. If you are intimidated by the idea of making pizza or pasta dough from scratch, this chapter is for you. But if you aren't afraid of anything at all, we challenge you to take on this book's most difficult recipe, the Timpano (p. 195).

Pro tip: complete your dinner party menu by mixing and matching dishes from this section with seasonally appropriate recipes from the Salads + Vegetables chapter.

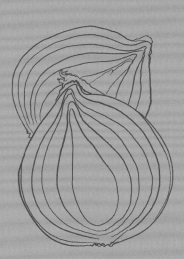

Fennel alla Romana with Shrimp

SERVES 4–6   **SPRING**

This is our take on the classic Roman dish puntarelle alla romana. The original dish is close to perfection, with thin, bitter curls of puntarelle (a member of the chicory family with long green-and-white shoots) front and center. We love bitter vegetables, but when spring finally pokes its head through our doors, it's nice to put bitterness aside for a moment and allow ourselves to experience some softness. That's why, in our version, we replaced the puntarelle with fennel and topped it with marinated wild-caught shrimps to sweeten the whole thing even more.

Marinate the shrimps: If you're using frozen shrimps, place them in a colander and thaw by running cold water over them. Peel the shrimps (keep the shells if you wish to make stock later). In a medium bowl, combine the shrimps, 2 tbps olive oil, the lemon zest, garlic and chilies. Cover and let the shrimps marinate in the fridge for at least 30 minutes and up to 1 day.

Cut and salt the fennel: Cut away any brown or dry-looking parts of the fennel, as well as ¼ inch off the bottom. Cut the bulbs in half through the core and, using a sharp knife, remove the core by cutting a triangle shape out of it. Cut the fennel lengthwise into thin strips and transfer to a large bowl. Sprinkle with 1½ tsp kosher salt and toss. Transfer to a large colander set over a bowl to drain for 1 hour.

Make the vinaigrette: In a small bowl, place the anchovies, red wine vinegar, white wine vinegar, sugar, garlic, olive oil and lemon juice. Whisk to combine until the sugar has dissolved.

Dress the fennel: Transfer the drained fennel to a large mixing bowl and toss in the vinaigrette and a few twists of pepper. Add the parsley, toss again, taste and adjust the seasoning with more lemon juice, salt and pepper if needed. Divide into bowls.

(continued)

Shrimp

1 lb (450 g) fresh or frozen wild-caught humpback or spot prawn shrimps

4 tbsp extra virgin olive oil, divided

Finely grated zest of 1 lemon

4 cloves garlic, finely grated

1 small fresh red chili (serrano or Espelette), thinly sliced

2 pinches kosher salt

Fennel Salad

2 lb (900 g) fennel (about 2 large bulbs)

1½ tsp kosher salt + more to season

Freshly ground black pepper

½ cup roughly chopped fresh parsley

2 tbsp fresh lemon juice (optional)

¾ cup Toasted Breadcrumbs (p. 251)

1 lemon, cut into wedges

Anchovy Vinaigrette

8–10 anchovy fillets, minced

2 tbsp red wine vinegar

4 tbsp white wine vinegar

½ tsp sugar

2–3 cloves garlic, minced

1¼ cups extra virgin olive oil

⅓ cup fresh lemon juice

Cook the shrimps and assemble the dish: Lightly season the shrimps with 2 pinches of salt. In a large frying pan, heat the remaining 2 tbsp olive oil over medium-high. Once the oil is hot and sizzling, distribute the shrimps in an even layer and turn off the heat immediately. After 30 seconds, flip the shrimps to cook the other side for about 30 seconds (note that larger shrimps will take longer to cook). Top the dressed fennel with the warm shrimps and seasoned breadcrumbs. Serve with a lemon wedge.

Charred Char with Chard

SERVES 4–6 SUMMER

We're pretty sure we initially wanted to make this dish just for the alliteration. But Janice being a magician in the kitchen, she turned a joke into a cookbook-worthy recipe, and that is no small feat. Arctic char is one of the best sustainable fish we can get our hands on in the winter, and rainbow chard is often the only way to get some greens in our lives during the colder months in Quebec. If you're up for a challenge, you can buy a whole char and fillet it yourself, but we personally recommend saving yourself the trouble by asking your fishmonger to do that for you.

Make the fennel condiment: In a wide, shallow pan, gently heat half of the olive oil on medium-low heat. Add the diced shallots and sweat for 3 minutes. Add the anchovies, garlic, chili flakes and pepper and continue cooking until the garlic becomes fragrant and is just beginning to change color, about 3 minutes. Add the fennel, tomato paste and salt and cook, stirring occasionally, for 10 more minutes. Add the remaining olive oil and continue cooking on low until the fennel is translucent, 5 minutes. (The oil should turn red and separate from the rest of the mixture.) Taste and adjust the seasoning with more salt and pepper. Leave in the pan and set aside.

Blanch the rainbow chard: Bring a large pot of salted water to a boil. Meanwhile, separate the rainbow chard stems and leaves and prepare a large bowl of ice water. Add the stems to the pot of boiling water and blanch them until just tender, but not soft, about 1 minute. Using tongs, remove the stems from the water and immediately plunge them in the bowl of ice water. Drain and chop on an angle into ¾-inch sticks. Set aside. Tear the leaves in half and set aside.

(continued)

Fennel Condiment

1½ cups extra virgin olive oil, divided

4 medium shallots, diced small

8 anchovy fillets

5 cloves garlic, minced

½ tsp dried chili flakes (or more if you like it very spicy)

¼ tsp freshly ground black pepper

1½ medium bulbs fennel, diced

3 tbsp tomato paste

1 tsp kosher salt

Chard and Char

1 medium bunch rainbow chard

2 arctic char fillets (each about 1 lb/450 g), cut in half

4 tbsp extra virgin olive oil, divided

1 tsp kosher salt + more to season

3 tbsp unsalted butter, divided

⅓ cup vegetable stock

1–2 tbsp fresh lemon juice, to taste

Flaky sea salt and freshly ground black pepper

1 lemon, cut into wedges

Char the char: Heat a large cast-iron skillet over medium-high heat. Coat the char fillets with 2 tbsp olive oil on both sides and season with the kosher salt. When the cooking surface is hot, add the remaining 2 tbsp oil and allow to heat for 10 seconds. Carefully lay the fish skin side down and cook until the skin is crispy and nicely charred, about 5 minutes. Add 1 tbsp butter to the pan and, using a flexible heatproof spatula or tongs, delicately turn the fillets over, then remove the pan from the heat.

Cook the chard leaves and fennel condiment: Heat the pan with the fennel condiment back up over medium heat. Add the chard leaves, chopped stems and vegetable stock. Cook until the leaves are tender and the stems are heated through, about 3 minutes. Stir in the remaining 2 tbsp butter and turn off the heat. Add the lemon juice. Taste and adjust the seasoning with kosher salt.

Assemble the dish: Transfer the fish to a serving plate and remove the skins. Spoon the fennel condiment and chard onto the plate. Sprinkle the fish with flaky sea salt, a few twists black pepper and serve with a lemon wedge.

Stuffed Roasted Fish with Olive Tapenade

SERVES 4–6   AUTUMN

This is such a fresh and light way to prepare fish, and once you've mastered the deboning technique, this dish also comes together very quickly. If you don't want to go through the trouble of deboning a fish yourself (it's a great kitchen skill to hone), just ask your fishmonger to remove the spine and bones for you or leave the bones and skin intact and remove them after cooking. Serve it with Beans, Beans, Beans (p. 49) and Cicoria alla Romana with Bottarga (p. 58).

Debone the fish: Using sharp scissors, cut the dorsal, pelvic and pectoral fins from one fish, leaving the tail and the head intact. Open up the fish and, starting from the neck, cut along one side of the spine, making sure not to go through the back end. Using your scissors, make a cut at the neckline to release the spine. Flip the fish and make the same long cut along the other side of the spine. Butterfly open the fish and, using your scissors, cut out the spine, starting from the severed neckline down to the tail. Next, insert your knife underneath the rib bones near the head and run it all the way down the side. Gently pull the rib bones out. Do the same with the ribs on the other side. Pick out all the remaining pin bones using your tweezers. Repeat with the other fish.

Preheat the oven and stuff the fish: Preheat the oven to 450°F and place a rack in the middle. Open up and season each fish with 4 tbsp olive tapenade and some salt and pepper. Stuff with a layer of onion slices, then a layer of lemon slices and lastly a layer of the fennel. Close up both fish by tying two strings near the belly of each, a few inches apart.

Roast: Place both fish in a baking dish. Rub the outside of each fish with ½ tbsp olive oil, and sprinkle with salt and pepper. Put the fish in the oven and roast until the internal temperature reads 145°F, 12–15 minutes.

Assemble and serve the fish: Leave in the baking dish or transfer to a platter, top with oven-dried tomatoes and drizzle with some olive oil. Serve with lemon wedges.

Special Equipment

Sharp scissors
Very sharp fish knife
Fish tweezers
4 (10-inch) pieces of string

Stuffed Fish

2 whole fish (each about 1–2 lb/450–900 g; we like European sea bass or sea bream)
8 tbsp Olive Tapenade (p. 268), divided
Kosher salt and freshly ground black pepper
1 small onion, thinly sliced
2 lemons, sliced
½ medium bulb fennel, thinly sliced (1 cup)
1 tbsp extra virgin olive oil, divided

Assembly

Oven-Dried Cherry Tomatoes (p. 265)
Extra virgin olive oil, to finish
1 lemon, cut into wedges

Dante Chicken Thighs

SERVES 4 SUMMER

Could we even call this a cookbook if we didn't include at least one grilled or roasted chicken recipe? We've never had a chicken dish on the menu at the restaurant, but we all love chicken. Everybody loves chicken! But we didn't want to write up a chicken recipe just for the sake of it. We wanted it to make sense for us and for you. That's why we decided to repurpose our Dante Vinegar (p. 264) as a marinade for the chicken. The vinegar not only helps tenderize the meat, but also keeps it from drying out. It's a one-stop brine and marinade shop! You will get tastier results using a charcoal grill (obviously), but the chicken will still be juicy and delicious cooked over medium on a gas grill.

Marinate the chicken: In a small bowl, place the Dante vinegar, 2 tbsp olive oil, kosher salt, onions and garlic. Toss to combine and set aside. In a large bowl, sprinkle the skin of the chicken thighs with the oregano and black pepper. Pour the marinade over the chicken and toss to coat. Marinate in the fridge for at least 1 hour and up to 2 days, flipping the thighs every once in a while.

Grill the chicken: Take the chicken thighs out of the fridge to temper for 30 minutes. Bring your grill up to medium-high heat. Remove the chicken thighs from the marinade and place them skin side up on the grill. Cook, gently flipping them after a nice color has developed, about 6–8 minutes. Cook the skin side carefully, allowing for a nice sear to develop before moving the meat to avoid tearing the skin, about 8 minutes. Finish cooking the thighs on the edge of the grill so the meat doesn't burn, flipping every once in a while, until the internal temperature reaches 160°F. Remove from the grill and rest for at least 8 minutes before cutting into it.

Grill the onions: While the chicken is resting, coat the onion quarters with the olive oil and season with salt and pepper. Grill on each side for about 3 minutes, until the onions are tender and nicely charred but still somewhat intact.

Assemble the dish: Plate the chicken thighs while they are still hot and top with a drizzle of olive oil, flaky sea salt and charred onions.

Grilled Chicken

⅓ cup Dante Vinegar (p. 264)

2 tbsp extra virgin olive oil + more to finish

1 tsp kosher salt

½ onion, sliced (about 1 cup)

7 cloves garlic, smashed

4 skin-on, bone-in chicken thighs

½ tsp dried oregano

¼ tsp freshly ground black pepper

Flaky sea salt

Grilled Onions

2 large onions, quartered

2 tbsp olive oil

½ tsp kosher salt

¼ tsp freshly ground black pepper

Porchetta with Peach Mostarda

SERVES 8–10   WINTER

What better way to say "I care about you" than by spending the weekend making a porchetta that's perfectly crispy on the outside and juicy on the inside? Sure, it takes a long time, but the look on your loved ones' faces when they take that first bite with a dollop of peach mostarda is well worth it. This recipe makes enough to feed at least eight people, so if you're not expecting a large group, we suggest using the leftovers to make Porchetta and Sage hoagies (p. 215) the next day.

Prepare the seasonings: Prepare three small bowls. In a dry frying pan, toast the fennel seeds, juniper berries and black peppercorns until fragrant, 2 minutes. Use a mortar and pestle or a small spice grinder to grind the spices together. Put the ground spices in the first bowl and toss in 3 tbsp salt. In the second bowl, place the lemon zest, garlic, rosemary, sage, parsley and 6 tbsp olive oil. Stir to combine. In the third bowl, combine 1 tbsp salt, the baking powder and the black pepper.

Score the skin: Set the pork belly skin side up. Using a very sharp knife or a utility blade, make lots of vertical cuts on the skin without going into the fat, about ½ inch apart. Take your time with this step, as it is crucial to achieve nice crispy skin.

Butterfly the belly and score the meat: Flip the belly so that the meat side is now facing up. Using a chef's knife, butterfly both ends of the belly horizontally where the meat is thickest to create more surface area for the seasoning. Next, score the meat in the center of the belly, creating ½-inch-deep cuts, 2 inches apart. This is going to allow the seasoning to penetrate deep into the meat.

Season the inside: Drizzle the cider all over the inside of the porchetta and massage it in with your hands. Sprinkle the toasted spice mixture all over the meat and massage again. Next, spread the chopped herb mixture all over the porchetta and rub it deep into the cuts.

Special Equipment

Mortar and pestle or small spice grinder

Very sharp knife or utility blade

Butcher's twine, cut into nine 18-inch pieces

Roasting pan with a rack

Porchetta

2 tbsp fennel seeds

2 tbsp juniper berries

1 tbsp black peppercorns

4 tbsp kosher salt, divided

Finely grated zest of 3 lemons

3–6 cloves garlic, minced

4 tbsp minced fresh rosemary

4 tbsp minced fresh sage

4 tbsp minced fresh parsley

6 tbsp extra virgin olive oil + more to season outside of porchetta

1 tbsp baking powder

2 tsp freshly ground black pepper

9 lb (4 kg) skin-on, deboned pork belly, cut 12 × 16 inches (ask your butcher for the thicker half of the belly where the loins and ribs were attached)

6 tbsp fortified cider or marsala

2 cups white wine

3–4 cups water

1–2 cups Peach Mostarda (p. 183), to serve to your liking

(continued)

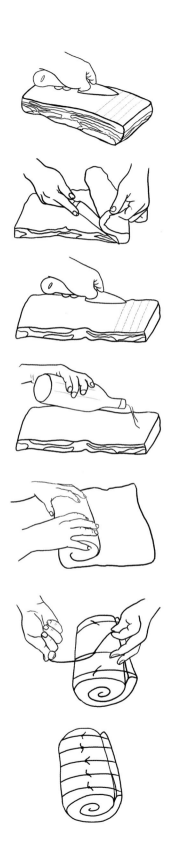

Roll and tie the porchetta: Fold the butterflied flaps back up and roll the belly as tight as you can, starting with the thickest part of the meat. Tie the roast with butcher's twine beginning in the center. Then tie both ends of the porchetta and work your way to the center, spacing each piece of twine by 2 inches. Snip off the excess twine.

Season the outside of the porchetta and chill: Place the porchetta on a roasting pan with a rack. Rub the skin with a little olive oil and the reserved salt, pepper and baking powder and chill the porchetta uncovered in the fridge overnight.

Temper the meat and preheat the oven: Remove the porchetta from the fridge 30 minutes before roasting. Preheat the oven to 500°F and set up a rack in the middle.

Roast the porchetta: Add the white wine and 3 cups water to the bottom of the roasting pan. Cook the porchetta in the oven until the skin becomes puffy and crispy, about 35 minutes.

Reduce the heat to 250°F and continue cooking for a total of 3 hours, adding more water to the pan if needed and checking the temperature every hour. The key to a tender roast is to reach and maintain an internal temperature of about 160°F–180°F, at which the collagen and fat in the pork belly will break down best, for 1–2 hours of the total cooking time.

Rest the porchetta and serve: Take the porchetta out of the oven and let it rest for at least 25 minutes before removing the twine. Cut it into nice thick slices and serve it warm with a dollop of peach mostarda. Store the leftover porchetta in an airtight container in the fridge and use it to make the Porchetta and Sage hoagie (p. 215) the next day.

Meatballs

SERVES 4 (MAKES 16 MEATBALLS)   ALL SEASONS

The meatballs at our other restaurant, Nora Gray, have been a staple on the menu since day one. When we opened Elena, we thought we would also do meatballs and that they, too, would become iconic. Even though they were delicious, it didn't really make sense for us to have them on the menu during an epic heatwave, so we took them off in our first year and kind of forgot about them. This recipe is for the woman who still comes to the restaurant asking for the meatballs we made for just a few weeks, four years ago. You know who you are, and you're welcome.

Make the breadcrumbs: In a food processor, pulse the bread pieces until the size of peas. Remove from the processor and set aside.

Sweat the vegetables: Place the onions, carrots and celery in the food processor and pulse until finely chopped. In a medium frying pan, heat the olive oil over medium heat. Add the finely chopped onions, carrots and celery and a generous pinch of kosher salt. Sweat until the vegetables have softened but not browned, about 10 minutes. Add the garlic and cook until fragrant, another 5 minutes. Transfer the vegetables to a large bowl and let cool completely, about 30 minutes.

Soak the breadcrumbs: Meanwhile, in a medium bowl, whisk to combine the milk and egg. Stir in the breadcrumbs and soak for 10 minutes.

Mix the meatballs: Preheat the oven to 400°F. Grab the bowl of cooled vegetables and add the pork, veal, beef, soaked breadcrumbs, parmesan, buffalo mozzarella, parsley, chili flakes, oregano, 1 tsp kosher salt and a few twists of pepper. Working with your hands, mix until the meat is completely combined with all the ingredients. Be careful not to overwork the meat—you want it to hold its shape without ever becoming too stiff. Heat a glug of olive oil in a small frying pan over medium-high heat. Cook a small chunk of the meatball mix to taste, and adjust the seasoning with more salt, black pepper or dried chili flakes.

Special Equipment
Food processor

1 cup roughly torn 1-inch pieces sourdough bread, crusts removed

½ medium onion, roughly chopped

½ carrot, peeled and roughly chopped

½ stalk celery, roughly chopped

2 tbsp extra virgin olive oil + more to test meatball seasoning

1 tsp kosher salt + more to season

1 large clove garlic, finely chopped

½ cup whole milk or buffalo mozzarella whey

1 large egg

½ lb (225 g) ground pork

¼ lb (113 g) ground veal

¼ lb (113 g) ground beef

2½ tbsp finely grated parmesan

1 ball (2½ oz/75 g or about ½ cup) buffalo mozzarella, crumbled (optional)

2½ tbsp finely chopped fresh parsley leaves

¼ tsp dried chili flakes

¼ tsp dried oregano

Freshly ground black pepper

7½ cups Tomato Sauce (p. 255)

(continued)

Roll out the meatballs: Wet your hands first to avoid any sticking. Divide the meat into 16 golf-ball-size portions and gently roll each into a ball between your palms. (Note: if you are making the Timpano on p. 195, divide the meat into 32 ping-pong-size balls.) It's OK if they aren't perfectly round, as long as they're about the same size. Space the meatballs evenly on a baking sheet.

Cook the meatballs: Bake the meatballs in the oven for 10 minutes. Meanwhile, in a large pot, heat the tomato sauce over medium-low heat. Taste the sauce and adjust the seasoning with more salt if needed, noting that as the meatballs cook, they will absorb some of the salt from the sauce. When the sauce is hot and the meatballs have come out of the oven, carefully add them one by one to the tomato sauce, making sure they are fully submerged. Cook for 20 minutes, keeping an eye on the temperature to avoid burning the tomato sauce.

Serve: Divide the meatballs into bowls and top with lots of tomato sauce. Serve the extra tomato sauce on the side (you'll thank us later).

Lamb Osso Bucco with Saffron Threads

SERVES 6–8   WINTER

This is our go-to for intimate dinner parties during the dead of winter. It's the kind of dish that looks super impressive on a table (slowly braised lamb with luxurious saffron threads) but that actually requires very little effort once you've done the initial step of salting the lamb the night before. Set it and forget it, then watch the compliments flood in.

Salt the lamb the night before: Place the lamb in a large dish or bowl and sprinkle the kosher salt all over. Cover the lamb and store in the fridge for at least 12 hours and up to 1 day. (In a pinch, you can salt the lamb just before cooking if you need to, but the texture of the meat is improved by salting the night before).

Preheat the oven and sear the lamb: Preheat the oven to 300°F. Pat the lamb pieces dry with a paper towel. In a large Dutch oven, heat the olive oil over medium heat. Once the oil is hot enough, working in batches, add the lamb shanks and sear on each side until golden, about 5 minutes per side. Remove the seared shanks and set aside. Turn off the heat but don't wipe the Dutch oven.

Warm up the chicken stock: While the shanks are searing, bring the chicken stock to a simmer in a medium pot over medium-high heat. Add the saffron threads and immediately turn off the heat. Set aside.

Cook the vegetables: In the same Dutch oven, add the onions, garlic, carrots, leeks, celery, bay leaves, chili flakes and pepper-corns. Cook over medium heat until fragrant and the vegetables have started to soften, 5 minutes. Stir in the tomato paste and cook for 2 minutes.

(continued)

Special Equipment
Immersion blender

Lamb Osso Bucco
4 lb (1.8 kg) lamb shanks, cut into 2 or 3 pieces depending on size

3 tbsp kosher salt

2 tbsp extra virgin olive oil

4 cups chicken stock

¼ tsp saffron threads

1 medium onion, cut into 1-inch pieces

10 cloves garlic, peeled and lightly crushed

2 carrots, peeled and cut into 1-inch pieces, or 4 whole Nantaise carrots

1 leek, cut into 1-inch chunks

1 stalk celery, cut into 1-inch chunks

3 bay leaves

½ tsp dried chili flakes

½ tsp black peppercorns

2 tbsp tomato paste

1 cup white wine

Creamy Polenta (p. 276), to serve

Cook the lamb: Add the shanks back to the Dutch oven, along with the white wine, and stir to deglaze the pot. Bring the wine to a simmer and cook until slightly reduced, 3 minutes. Add the warm saffron chicken stock and bring to a simmer. Cover and transfer to the oven. Cook until the meat is tender, 2½–3 hours.

Blend the sauce: Carefully remove the pot from the oven and use tongs or a slotted spoon to remove the meat and bay leaves. Set the lamb shanks aside and discard the bay leaves. Use an immersion blender to eliminate the bigger chunks from the sauce and smooth it out.

Serve: Divide the shanks onto plates, top with the sauce and serve with a side of creamy polenta.

Stek! With Pepperonata

No matter how good your restaurant is, if you're always working and you eat all of your meals there, you will eventually get sick of the food. A few months after opening Elena, Marley began campaigning every single day for Janice to put a steak on the menu because he was hungry for steak. Steph and Ryan eventually joined the movement, shouting "Stek!" whenever they could, giving Janice no other option but to come up with this incredible bavette with pepperonata dish to shut them up. This recipe comes together very quickly once the meat has marinated long enough to absorb all the aromatics, making it a great weeknight dinner.

Marinate the bavette: In a medium bowl, toss together the rosemary, olive oil and garlic. Add the bavette and toss until well coated. Transfer to a sealed container and refrigerate for at least 2 hours and up to 12 hours. Bring the meat to room temperature before cooking.

Roast and steam the peppers: Preheat the oven to 450°F and line a baking sheet with parchment paper. Place the peppers on the baking sheet and coat them lightly with 1 tsp olive oil. Bake until the peppers are charred around the edges, turning them halfway, about 20 minutes. Place the peppers inside a covered container to cool and steam for 30 minutes. When the peppers feel cool enough to handle, remove the skins, cores, seeds and stems. Slice them into ½-inch-wide strips.

Sear the bavette: In a large cast-iron skillet over medium-high heat, heat a glug of vegetable oil until almost smoking. Pat the bavette dry with a paper towel, then generously season both sides with salt and pepper. Add the bavette to the pan and reduce the heat to medium. Sear on both sides until the internal temperature reaches 135°F–140°F, 5–7 minutes each side. Remove the steak from the skillet and let it rest while you cook the pepperonata. Drain the excess oil but don't wash the pan.

Bavette

3 tbsp chopped fresh rosemary (roughly 3 sprigs)

½ cup extra virgin olive oil

2 cloves garlic, smashed

1¾ lb (800 g) bavette (flank steak)

Vegetable oil

Kosher salt

Freshly ground black pepper

Pepperonata

4 bell peppers (multicolor)

1 tsp + 2 tbsp extra virgin olive oil, divided

2 tbsp unsalted butter

1 small onion, thinly sliced

1 fresh red chili pepper, sliced

2–3 cloves garlic, thinly sliced

3 tbsp chopped fresh rosemary

1 cup red wine

2½ tbsp red wine vinegar

Chopped fresh parsley

Kosher salt and freshly ground black pepper

Assembly

Extra virgin olive oil

Flaky sea salt

Freshly ground black pepper

(continued)

Cook the pepperonata: Heat the skillet back up over medium heat and add the butter and 2 tbsp olive oil. Cook until the butter is hot. Add the onions, chili peppers, garlic and rosemary. Sweat until the garlic is cooked and fragrant, but not burnt, 1 minute. Dump in all the peppers and the red wine and cook until the sauce is hot and has reduced slightly, 5–8 minutes. Turn off the heat, add the red wine vinegar and parsley, and season generously with salt and pepper.

Assemble: Slice the steak and arrange nicely on a platter. Top with the pepperonata. Finish with some olive oil, flaky sea salt and a few twists of pepper.

Timpano

SERVES 10–12   ALL SEASONS

If you've ever watched the movie *Big Night*, then you already know what a timpano is. If you haven't, a timpano is basically a very elaborate, medieval-looking lasagna. We also consider this recipe as our cookbook's final boss because in order to make it, you need to have mastered other recipes found within these pages, such as the egg pasta dough, the tomato sauce, the meatballs and the fried eggplant. It's also a great way to use the leftovers. This dish requires a lot of steps and is by no means easy to make, which is why we suggest you read it from start to finish at least three times over (including all the subrecipes) before you even begin prepping. You don't want to start making a timpano only to realize you're missing half the ingredients or forgot to prepare something that takes 2 hours to make. This recipe yields a very large amount, perfect for a large party.

Day 1

Make the tomato sauce: Double the recipe on p. 255 and follow the instructions, adding an extra 5 tsp kosher salt, ¾ tsp oregano, ¾ freshly ground black pepper, ¾ dried chili flakes and 12 torn basil leaves. You will be using half of the sauce to cook the meatballs (see next step) and half to assemble and serve the timpano.

Make the meatballs: Follow the instructions on p. 185, but divide the meat into 32 ping-pong-size meatballs instead of 16 golf-ball-size meatballs (we love sports!).

Boil the eggs: Prepare a bowl of ice water. Bring a medium pot of water to a boil. Add 10 room-temperature eggs and boil for 7 minutes. Remove the eggs and transfer to the ice bath. Once they're cool enough to handle, peel them. Store the eggs in a water-filled container and refrigerate until ready to use.

(continued)

Special Equipment

6-quart Dutch oven (11-inch diameter)

Spray bottle

Rolling pin

Large cutting board (a few inches larger than the Dutch oven)

Tomato Sauce

2 batches Tomato Sauce (p. 255)

5 tsp kosher salt

¾ tsp dried oregano

¾ tsp freshly ground black pepper

¾ tsp dried chili flakes

12 leaves fresh basil, torn

Filling

1 batch Meatballs (p. 185), shaped into 32 ping-pong-size balls

14 large eggs, room temperature (10 for boiling, 4 raw)

2 batches Fried Eggplant (p. 206)

Flaky sea salt, to season eggs

1 lb (450 g) pasta (store-bought penne or rigatoni)

⅛ tsp freshly ground pepper

¼ tsp kosher salt

1½ cups grated parmesan

4 balls (10½ oz/300 g or about 2 cups) buffalo mozzarella, each cut into 8 pieces

3 cups grated auricchio (spicy provolone)

Dough

5 cups all-purpose flour + more for dusting

2 large eggs

12 large egg yolks

1 tsp kosher salt

4 tbsp water

6 tbsp extra virgin olive oil, divided

Assembly and serving

Enough salted butter to grease the inside of a Dutch oven

2 tbsp extra virgin olive oil, to finish

Flaky sea salt, to finish

Make the dough: Follow the instructions on p. 127 to make the dough but using the quantities listed to the left. Rest the dough at room temperature for at least 30 minutes before using.

Fry the eggplant: Follow the instructions on p. 206 and set aside.

Reheat the meatballs: In a large pot, lightly reheat the meatballs in the sauce, adding ¼ cup water to loosen it slightly. Remove from the heat and set aside.

Prepare the eggs: Remove the hard-boiled eggs from the water and cut them in half lengthwise. Season them lightly with flaky sea salt.

Cook the pasta: Bring a large pot of salted water to a boil. Cook the pasta to half the recommended cooking time. Strain, then toss in 2½ cups tomato sauce. Spread on a baking sheet to cool.

Beat the remaining eggs: In a small bowl, beat the remaining 4 eggs with ⅛ tsp pepper and ¼ tsp salt. Set aside.

Preheat the oven and set up your filling ingredients: Preheat the oven to 350°F. Before you start rolling the dough, triple check you have all of your filling ingredients ready to go.

Line the Dutch oven: Grease the Dutch oven with salted butter and set aside.

Roll out the dough: Rolling the dough is a long process, so have a spray bottle filled with water on hand to make sure the dough doesn't dry out. Lightly flour a large, clean work surface like a dining table. Using a large rolling pin, roll out the pasta dough into a 30-inch-diameter circle. Do this gradually by rotating the dough, working one section at a time (patience is key). If the dough feels too tough, rest it, covered, for a few minutes. Stop when you have gotten to roughly 30 inches in diameter. Brush 2 tbsp olive oil onto each side of the rolled dough. Carefully fold it in half on itself once, then do it again. Place the twice-folded dough in the greased Dutch oven, positioning the corner in the center of the pot, and carefully unfold until the dough is evenly draped over the Dutch oven. Gently press the dough against the inside wall, careful not to break it. The dough should hang over the edge of the Dutch oven by about 4 inches all around.

Layer the timpano filling: Spread 1½ cups tomato sauce on the bottom of the dough. Add a layer of saucy cooked pasta to fill the bottom, arranging them beautifully. (Keep in mind how things will look when you cut into the timpano.) Then layer the rest of the ingredients in this order:

- ¼ cup parmesan
- ½ of the mozzarella chunks
- 16 meatballs (fill any gaps with pasta)
- 10 boiled egg halves
- 1 cup auricchio
- ¼ cup parmesan
- 1½ cups tomato sauce
- All the fried eggplant
- ¼ cup parmesan
- 1½ cups tomato sauce
- 1 cup auricchio
- ¼ cup parmesan

- Another layer of pasta
- ¼ cup parmesan
- The remaining mozzarella chunks
- The rest of the meatballs (fill the holes)
- The rest of the eggs
- 1 cup auricchio
- ¼ cup parmesan
- 1½ cups tomato sauce
- The beaten eggs (poured over everything)

Close the timpano: Fold the dough up toward the center, with as little overlap as possible (trim the dough as you go so you don't end up with too many thick layers). Make sure the dough is well sealed up by using a bit of water to pinch the openings shut.

Bake the timpano: Cover and place the Dutch oven on a baking sheet and roast for an hour. Remove the cover and cook until the dough turns a light brown color, about 30 minutes. Take out of the oven and let it sit for at least 30 minutes.

Unmold: Ask a friend to help you for this next step because the timpano will be very heavy at this point. To unmold, place a large cutting board (it should be a few inches wider than the Dutch oven) over the top. Grab the handles of the Dutch oven, firmly hold the cutting board down, and flip the whole thing over. Carefully lift the Dutch oven from the cutting board. Let it rest for at least another 45 minutes before cutting it. This is really important.

Serve: Reheat your leftover tomato sauce. Brush the outside of the timpano with 2 tbsp olive oil and top with a generous pinch of flaky sea salt. Cut the slices and serve with tomato sauce.

BECOMING YOUR BEST SELF IS LIKE BUILDING A TIMPANO

By Stephanie Mercier Voyer

Whenever I used to think about how I could become the best version of myself, I would often focus on all the little things I wish I could change, sometimes even wishing I was a different person altogether. But now when I think about becoming my best self, I think about making a timpano.

Hear me out. Becoming a better person is not about tucking away pieces of yourself and pretending you're somebody different. It's about seeing all the weird bits that make you *you*—your qualities, your flaws, your family and your friends—and believing that with some self-work and acceptance, you can combine those bits and feel like a whole person. It's a lot of work but it's a labor of love.

Building a timpano feels just like that. It requires you to combine a bunch of recipes that might not seem to be a great fit at first, including ingredients that are somewhat imperfect (like a broken meatball) or things you maybe wish you didn't have (leftovers). Successfully making a timpano demands your full attention and complete trust in the process. You have to believe that at the end of the day, all the weird bits, from the fried eggplant to the hard-boiled eggs, will come together (thanks to multiple layers of cheese and lots of patience) to create a gigantic timpano that you can share with all the people who love you for you.

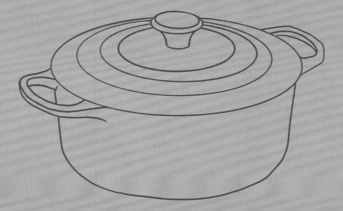

HOAGIES

A great hoagie is like a loving, supporting community because a great hoagie is a lot more than the sum of its parts. From the buns to the shredded radicchio, every ingredient in our hoagies could stand on its own and bring something unique to the table. But it's when they come together that the real magic happens. Sure, mortadella would taste great in any old sandwich, but how do you really make it sing? In our mortadella hoagie, we choose to highlight the meat's richness by contrasting it with a high-acid giardiniera mix that's made with some of the summer's most beautiful vegetables. How do you go about breathing new life into yesterday's porchetta? We like to lean in to the comfort-food vibes and pair our thinly sliced leftovers with homemade sage-infused mayonnaise and pickled honey mushrooms.

That's the approach we take with everything we do in life—whether it's an artist collaboration for a new T-shirt, buying produce from a local farm or doing a pop-up with our friend's restaurant. We always want to find new ways to make the people around us shine. At the risk of sounding cheesy, we wouldn't be where we are now if it weren't for our community. And in a weird way, we wouldn't still be here if it weren't for hoagies.

Right before the pandemic started, our pizzaiolo, Chris, took a trip down to Philadelphia to eat at Pizzeria Beddia. We thought that when he came back, he wouldn't shut up about the pizza,

but instead, the only thing on his mind was the hoagies. So when everything shut down a few months later, and we had no idea what was going to happen with the restaurant, Chris's initial reaction was to start pickling everything. There was no stopping him. He made so many pickles that, eventually, we had to figure out a way to use them—and so the Elena hoagie was born. We started to sell them during lunch, and people just couldn't get enough. They became almost as popular as our pizza and allowed us to stay afloat during the darkest days of lockdown.

We always say that good things happen when people come together. And great hoagies are made when good ingredients come together. But when good people and great hoagies come together, we can survive almost anything—even a global pandemic.

In this chapter, we share a few recipes in which all sorts of ingredients come together to create powerhouse hoagies. You will also learn how to make our hoagie bun, complete with our very special hoagie spice mix. But rest assured, you can still recreate these sandwiches without baking your own bread. Just make sure to buy high-quality 10- to 12-inch-long buns.

Hoagie Bun

MAKES 1 HOAGIE BUN

1 ball Neapolitan Pizza Dough
(p. 69 or 70)

½ cup semolina rimacinata

1 large egg

1 tbsp water

2 tbsp Hoagie Spice Mix
(p. 253)

We love these buns because we make them with the same dough balls we use for our Neapolitan pizza. This means that if you make a big batch of dough, you can divide it and shape a few balls for pizza and a few others for hoagies. When you're ready to cut your buns to assemble your hoagie, make sure to keep the back seam of the bun attached. It will make it easier to close your sandwich without any of the ingredients spilling out.

Temper the dough: Remove the dough from the fridge and temper for a minimum of 20 minutes on the counter.

Shape the dough: Lightly oil a baking sheet and set aside. Using a dough scraper, carefully transfer the tempered dough into a mound of semolina. Flip the dough and flour the other side. Transfer the dough to a clean surface and gently shape it into a square. To stretch the dough so that it takes the rectangular shape of a hoagie, pick up the dough square with your hands and let it hang down, moving your hands along it as if you were climbing a rope in reverse, and allow gravity to work its magic. Continue stretching the dough until it is about 8 inches long and 3 inches wide. Put the stretched hoagie dough on the oiled baking sheet, seam side facing down, and let it proof, uncovered, at room temperature for 20 minutes.

Preheat the oven and beat the egg: Preheat the oven to 475°F. In a small bowl, crack the egg, then add the water and beat until homogeneous. Set aside.

Bake the hoagie bun: Brush the top of the proofed dough with the beaten egg wash, then sprinkle with the hoagie spice mix. Bake the hoagie bun until lightly golden brown, about 12–15 minutes.

Mortadella

This is our benchmark hoagie. It hits all the right notes. You get a lot of umami flavors from the sharp provolone, and the giardiniera cuts right through the richness of the mortadella. It's the perfect sandwich.

Mix the lettuce: In a small bowl, toss to combine the shredded iceberg lettuce and radicchio. Set aside.

Assemble the hoagie: Cut the bun lengthwise, making sure not to cut through the other side. Spread the mustard on the top side of the bun and mayonnaise on the bottom. On the top side of the bun, add the shredded lettuce and giardiniera. On the bottom side, add the mortadella followed by the shaved auricchio. Close the hoagie and cut it in half for a more manageable bite.

¼ cup shredded iceberg lettuce

¼ cup shredded radicchio

1 Hoagie Bun (p. 204)

1½ tbsp Hoagie Mustard (p. 260)

2 tbsp Hoagie Mayonnaise (p. 259)

½ cup Giardiniera (p. 281)

¼ lb (113 g) sliced mortadella

¼ cup shaved auricchio (spicy provolone)

Eggplant Parmesan

MAKES 1 HOAGIE   SUMMER

Fried Eggplant

1 small eggplant, cut into ½-inch disks (about 5 slices)

1½ tbsp kosher salt

½ cup all-purpose flour

1 large egg, beaten

1 tbsp water

1 cup Seasoned Breadcrumbs (p. 252)

Vegetable oil, enough for frying

Hoagie

1 Hoagie Bun (p. 204)

¼ cup Garlic Butter (p. 277)

8 tbsp Tomato Sauce (p. 255), divided

2 slices provolone, cut in half

½ ball (1.3 oz/38 g or about ¼ cup) buffalo mozzarella, sliced

6 leaves fresh basil

¼ cup grated parmesan

You could make the fried eggplant with parmesan and tomato sauce and serve it with our Kale! Caesar! (p. 29) and it would be delicious. But the only real way to elevate eggplant parmesan, in our opinion, is to put it in a sandwich.

Prepare the eggplant: Line a baking sheet with paper towel and place the eggplant slices on the sheet. Season them with the salt and let them sit for 30 minutes to allow some of the excess water to come out. Pat them dry with paper towel.

Preheat the oven and prepare the breading ingredients: Preheat the oven to broil (500°F). Prepare three small bowls. Put the flour in the first bowl. In the second bowl, thin out the eggs by whisking in 1 tbsp water. In the third bowl, put the seasoned breadcrumbs.

Bread the eggplant slices: Working one slice at a time, drop the eggplant in the flour and shake off the excess. Dip it into the egg mixture and let the excess drip off. Next, roll it into the breadcrumb bowl, pressing the crumbs firmly in the eggplant, and put on an unlined baking sheet (if using the same baking sheet, remove the paper towels and dry the baking sheet). Repeat with the remaining eggplant slices until they are all breaded.

Fry the eggplant: Add enough frying oil to a cast-iron skillet to reach a depth of ⅓ inch, and heat it over medium-high heat. Check if the oil is hot enough by adding a pinch of breadcrumbs—if it sputters, it means the oil is ready for frying. Using tongs, add the breaded eggplant slices to the hot oil and fry until golden brown, about 3 minutes on each side, reducing the heat if you notice the eggplant coloring too quickly. Transfer the fried eggplant onto a clean baking sheet lined with paper towel to absorb any excess oil. Season lightly with salt and set aside.

Assemble the hoagie: Cut the bun lengthwise, making sure not to cut through the other side. Spread the garlic butter on the top and bottom sides of the bun, then add 2 tbsp tomato sauce on the bottom. Add the fried eggplant slices and spoon the rest of the tomato sauce over them. Top with the provolone slices.

Toast the hoagie: Put the hoagie, face open, on a baking sheet and broil in the oven until the cheese begins to melt and the top bun starts to take on some color, about 2–3 minutes. Remove from the oven and transfer to a cutting board.

Finish and cut the hoagie: Top the eggplant side with the mozzarella slices and basil leaves. Sprinkle everything with grated parmesan. Close the bun and cut the hoagie in half.

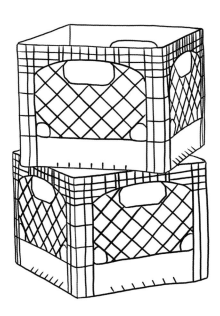

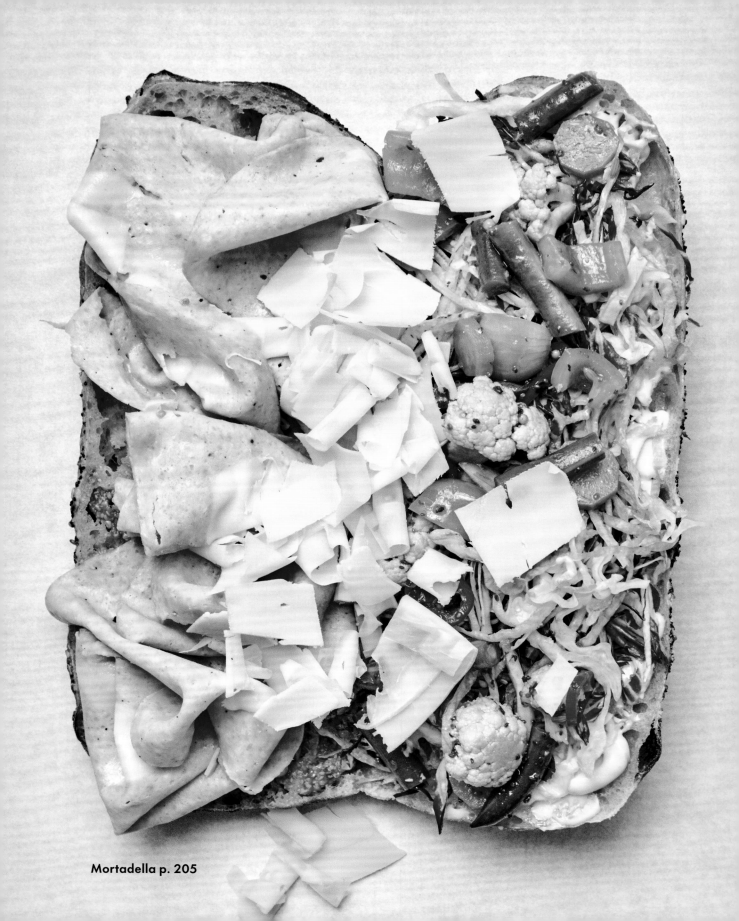

Mortadella p. 205

Eggplant Parmesan p. 206

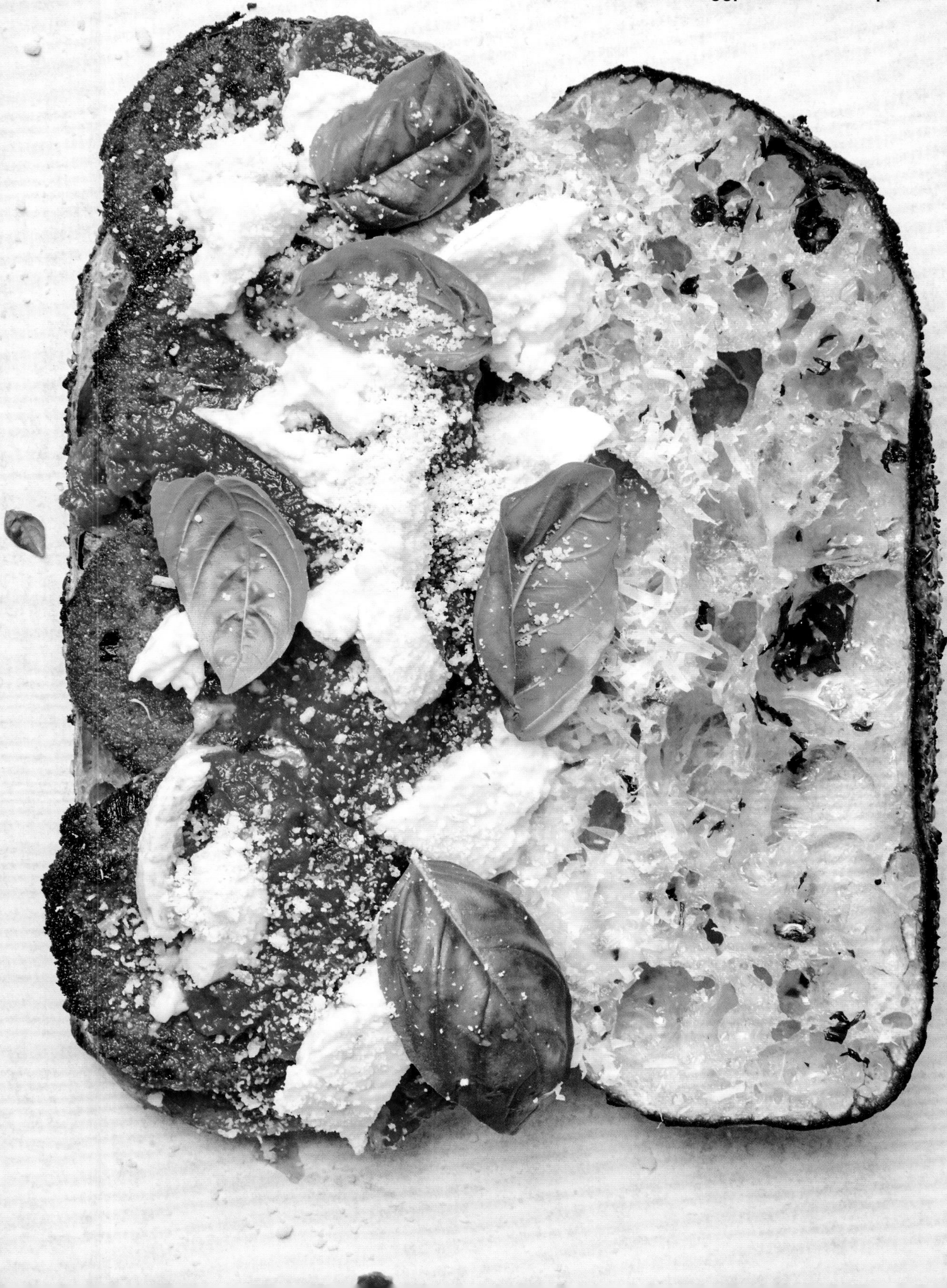

Dr. Lyle

Our friend Nick Hodge at Sugaree Farm grows these super-savory and beefy heirloom tomatoes from seeds that have been passed down from Nick's family by a man named Dr. Lyle. Since they're almost impossible to get, we suggest you make this hoagie using a dense and savory variety of heirloom tomato you might find at the market, or beefsteak tomatoes. We're sure Dr. Lyle wouldn't mind.

Assemble the hoagie: Cut the bun lengthwise, making sure not to cut through the other side. Spread the mayonnaise on the top side of the bun and the olive tapenade on the bottom. On the top side of the bun, add the mozzarella slices and basil leaves. On the bottom side, add the tomato slices, followed by the pickles. Sprinkle with flaky sea salt and a few twists of pepper. Close the bun, cut it in half and enjoy right away.

1 Hoagie Bun (p. 204)

3 tbsp Hoagie Mayonnaise (p. 259)

3 tbsp Olive Tapenade (p. 268)

½ ball (1.3 oz/38 g or about ¼ cup) buffalo mozzarella, sliced

5 leaves fresh basil

1 heirloom tomato, sliced

5 slices Bread and Butter Pickles (p. 287)

Flaky sea salt

Freshly ground black pepper

Sausage Spigarello p. 214

Porchetta and Sage p. 215

Sausage Spigarello

MAKES 1 HOAGIE WINTER

Spigarello

3 tbsp extra virgin olive oil + more after greens are cooked

2 cloves garlic, thinly sliced

1 small chili, thinly sliced, or 1 pinch dried chili flakes

Kosher salt

2 tbsp white wine

2 cups spigarello, rapini or dandelion greens, washed, tough stems removed and roughly chopped

Freshly ground black pepper

Sausage

1 tbsp extra virgin olive oil

½ batch Fennel Sausage (p. 115), shaped into one long patty or 2 smaller ones

Hoagie

1 Hoagie Bun (p. 204)

3 tbsp Hoagie Mayonnaise (p. 259)

¼ cup shaved aged provolone

5 slices provolone

2½ tbsp Pepperoncini (p. 286)

Move over rapini, there's a new green kid in town. Spigarello, an Italian heirloom variety from the brassica family, is one of our favorite greens to cook with because it's not quite as bitter as other winter greens, but still feels hearty. This is essentially the hoagie version of our sausage pizza (p. 115)—both are delicious, but this one's a lot easier to stash in a backpack for your next hike.

Cook the spigarello: Bring a large pot of salted water to a boil. In a large skillet, heat the olive oil over medium heat, then add the sliced garlic, chili and a generous pinch of salt. Cook until the garlic is fragrant and just beginning to turn golden, 2 minutes. Deglaze the pan with white wine and continue to cook to reduce the liquid slightly while you blanch the greens. Add the spigarello to the pot of boiling water and cook for 1 minute. Use tongs or a strainer to transfer the blanched greens to the pan. Add a pinch of salt and a few twists of pepper and cook until the greens are tender and most of the liquid has been absorbed, 2–5 minutes. Add an extra glug of olive oil, taste and adjust the seasoning as needed.

Fry the sausage: Heat a cast-iron skillet over medium-high heat and add 1 tbsp olive oil. Heat the olive oil for 30 seconds, then sear the sausage patty for 2 minutes on each side. Transfer to a plate and set aside.

Assemble the hoagie: Cut the bun lengthwise, making sure not to cut through the other side. Spread the mayonnaise on both sides of the bun. On the bottom side, add the sauteed spigarello, warm sausage, provolone and pepperoncini. Close the bun tightly and cut the hoagie in half before eating.

Porchetta and Sage

MAKES 1 HOAGIE   WINTER

There are 1,001 reasons why you'd want to make a porchetta for one (you're really hungry, you love a challenge, there's a global pandemic and you are trapped inside for months on end, etc.). But our personal favorite reason to do so is just to make sure that we have enough leftovers to make this hoagie. Porchetta for one, sandwiches for days.

Mix the lettuce: In a medium bowl, toss to combine the iceberg and radicchio, and set aside.

Assemble the hoagie: Cut the hoagie bun lengthwise, making sure not to cut through the other side. Spread sage mayonnaise on the inside top part of the bun and mustard on the inside bottom. Spread the lettuce mix on the mayonnaise side and evenly distribute the porchetta slices on the mustard side. Add the pickled honey mushrooms over the lettuce and top the meat with the sage leaves. Close up the hoagie and cut it in half for a more manageable eating experience or to share with a friend.

¼ cup shredded iceberg lettuce

¼ cup shredded radicchio

1 Hoagie Bun (p. 204)

3 tbsp Sage Mayonnaise (p. 259)

1 tbsp Hoagie Mustard (p. 260)

4 thin slices (about 3½ oz/100 g) Porchetta (p. 183)

½ cup Pickled Honey Mushrooms (p. 283)

6 leaves fresh sage

Meatball Hero p. 218

Meatball Hero

MAKES 1 HOAGIE   ALL SEASONS

¼ cup shredded iceberg lettuce

¼ cup shredded radicchio

1 Hoagie Bun (p. 204)

¼ cup Garlic Butter (p. 277), room temperature

½ cup Tomato Sauce (p. 255), divided

3 slices provolone, cut in half

½ ball (1.3 oz/38 g or about ¼ cup) buffalo mozzarella, sliced

4 Meatballs (p. 185)

1–2 tbsp Pepperoncini (p. 286) or pickled banana peppers (depending on desired spiciness)

5 leaves fresh basil

2 tbsp grated parmesan

Flaky sea salt

The term "hero" is generally used to describe hot or cold sub sandwiches. But the name feels especially fitting for this one. During the first few months of the pandemic, when we weren't sure if the restaurant could survive another week of lockdown, we would make a big batch of these hoagies. People were so obsessed with them that they would sell out instantly. In true hero fashion, the meatball hoagie would save the day every time. For your purposes, this recipe is a great way to breathe new life into your leftover meatballs.

Preheat the oven and mix the lettuce: Preheat the oven to broil (500°F). In a small bowl, toss to combine the shredded iceberg lettuce and radicchio. Set aside.

Assemble the hoagie: Cut the bun lengthwise, making sure not to cut through the other side. Spread the garlic butter on the top and bottom sides of the bun, then add 2 tbsp tomato sauce on the bottom. Add the provolone and buffalo mozzarella slices. Lightly press on the meatballs to flatten them a little, then place them over the cheeses and cover them with the remaining tomato sauce.

Toast the hoagie: Put the hoagie on a baking sheet and broil in the oven until the cheese begins to melt and the top bun starts to take on some color, 2–3 minutes. Remove from the oven and transfer to a cutting board.

Finish and cut the hoagie: On the top side of the bun, add the shredded lettuce and pepperoncini. Top the meatballs with the basil leaves, and sprinkle everything with the grated parmesan and a pinch of flaky sea salt. Close the hoagie, wrap it in kraft paper (optional), cut it in half and enjoy immediately (not optional).

Chicken Caesar

MAKES 1 HOAGIE **SUMMER**

You loved our kale salad in a bowl, now try it in a bun. The Kale! Caesar! (p. 29) has been one of the most popular items on our menu since the day we opened, which is why we decided to put it inside a sandwich along with juicy, sliced fried chicken. This may be a controversial opinion, but we think that this hoagie might be even better than the salad version.

Prepare the chicken: Cut the chicken breast or thigh lengthwise, making sure not to cut through the other side, and butterfly it open to create a flatter piece of meat that will cook more evenly. Set aside.

Preheat the oven and prepare the breading ingredients: Preheat the oven to broil (500°F). Prepare three small bowls. Put the flour in the first bowl. In the second bowl, thin out the eggs by whisking in 1 tbsp water. In the third bowl, put the seasoned breadcrumbs.

Bread the chicken: Drop the chicken in the flour and shake off the excess. Dip it into the egg mixture and let the excess drip off. Next, roll it in the breadcrumb bowl, pressing the crumbs firmly into the chicken, and set aside.

Fry the chicken: Add enough frying oil to a cast-iron skillet to reach a depth of ⅓ inch, and heat the oil over medium-high heat. Check if the oil is hot enough by adding a pinch of breadcrumbs—if it sputters, it means the oil is ready for frying. Using tongs, add the breaded chicken to the hot oil and fry until golden brown, about 2 minutes on each side, reducing the heat if you notice the chicken coloring too quickly. Transfer the chicken to a plate lined with paper towel to absorb any excess oil. Season lightly with salt and set aside.

(continued)

Fried Chicken
1 skinless boneless chicken breast or thigh
½ cup all-purpose flour
2 large eggs, beaten
1 tbsp water
1¼ cups Seasoned Breadcrumbs (p. 252)
Vegetable oil, enough for frying
Kosher salt

Hoagie
1 Hoagie Bun (p. 204)
¼ cup Garlic Butter (p. 277)
¼ cup shredded iceberg lettuce
¼ cup shredded radicchio
¼ cup shredded Tuscan kale
¼ cup Tahini Caesar Dressing (p. 29)
Juice of 1 lemon
¼ cup grated parmesan, divided
Flaky sea salt and freshly ground black pepper
1 heirloom tomato, sliced
1 tbsp Pickled Shallots (optional, p. 280)

Toast the bun: Cut the bun lengthwise, making sure not to cut through the other side. Spread the garlic butter on the top and bottom sides of the bun. Toast in the oven until the bun starts to take on some color, about 2–3 minutes. Remove from the oven and transfer to a cutting board.

Mix the greens: In a small bowl, toss to combine the shredded iceberg lettuce, radicchio and kale. Add the Caesar dressing, most of the lemon juice, half of the parmesan and the flaky sea salt and pepper to taste. Toss to fully coat the greens. Set aside.

Assemble the hoagie: Cut the chicken on a bias into three pieces and arrange on the bottom side of the bun so that each bite has a nice succulent layer of chicken without being stacked too much. Drizzle with the remaining lemon juice. Add the tomato slices, pickled shallots and dressed greens. Finish with the remaining parmesan. Close the hoagie, cut in half and enjoy!

PICTURE A SNAKE

Picture a Snake is a game we've been playing since Steph heard this guy give the absolute worst physical description of a raccoon to someone who had never seen one before. His description was so off, he might as well have said, "OK, so picture a snake, but instead of being a snake, it has four legs, no scales, a tiny bear face and a bushy tail about yea big." Since then, Picture a Snake has evolved into a metaphor about restaurants and a choose-your-own-adventure game we like to play to show that, with enough imagination, you can take even the simplest concepts (like a straight-line snake or opening a pizza restaurant) and turn them into something wilder and bigger than what you could have ever envisioned in the first place.

Making naturally leavened pizza in a wood-fire oven was our snake. Then we found a brown-bricked building, which we gutted and completely transformed into a brightly colored modern Italian room with lots of texture and natural light. We hired wonderful humans to work with us. We wrote a menu comprising salads, pizza, pasta, meat, fish, desserts and wine. We built a coffee shop around back, a terrasse, and then another terrasse. We planted a garden and two pear trees. People started coming and we made lots of new friends. We collaborated with artists to create a line of merch, including T-shirts, bags, hats, socks, water bottles, croakies, scrunchies and more. We started making hoagies and doing takeout. What started as a simple pizza snake has now become a community that keeps on growing.

Now it's time for you to grab a pen and start working on your very own snake. We asked our friend and illustrator Emilie Campbell to draw a few to give you some inspiration, but in the end, it's up to you to figure out where that snake will take you.

ROOSTER

HORSE

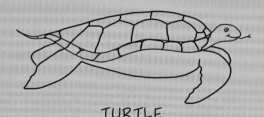

TURTLE

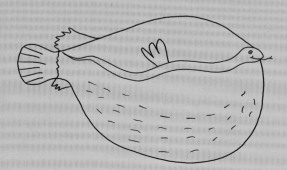

BLOWFISH

DESSERTS

We think you should wrap up every meal the way you want to end most things in life: on a high note. Whether it's a relationship or a dinner party, the way you leave things matters. It's how most people will remember you. That's not to say that endings are easy. They can be really, really difficult—just like baking.

In this chapter, we've included some of the best desserts we've ever made at the restaurant and others we've developed just for this book with the help of the über-talented pastry chef Michelle Marek. Some of these recipes, like the Pistachio Cookies (p. 231), are dangerously easy to make, like ending things with someone you've gone on one date with. Others, like the Babamisu (p. 243), require more technique and patience, like telling someone you still deeply care about that you've fallen out of love.

Endings are hard, but there are a lot of silver linings that come with letting go of things that aren't serving you anymore—like realizing you have a lot more time to enjoy the sweet things in life, whether that's a tart, a cake or new friends.

Mousse di Bufala with Rhubarb and Wildflowers

MAKES 6–8, DEPENDING ON THE SIZE OF YOUR MOLDS   SPRING

Finally, a dessert you won't feel guilty eating for breakfast. This yogurt mousse feels like a light panna cotta and tastes like springtime, thanks to the rhubarb and wildflower syrup.

Mix the mousse base: In a small pot, combine the milk, honey and sugar and bring to a boil. Immediately turn off the heat when the milk is boiling. While the milk is heating up, combine the gelatin and cold water in a small bowl. Let it rest until it has formed a mass and become solid, about 5 minutes. Once the milk has boiled and you have turned off the heat, add the gelatin to the hot milk mixture and whisk vigorously until it has fully dissolved. Place the yogurt in a medium bowl and pour the hot gelatin and milk mixture on top. Whisk to combine and set aside to cool to room temperature.

Whip the cream and make the mousse: Using a hand mixer or a whisk, whip the cream in a medium bowl until medium peaks form. When the mousse base has cooled down, fold in the whipped cream until homogeneous. Divide the mousse mixture into 6–8 molds or ramekins and refrigerate for at least 3 hours.

Cook the rhubarb and wildflowers: In a medium pot, bring the water, honey and sugar to a boil. Add the rhubarb and simmer for about 1 minute. Turn off the heat and add the wildflowers. Cover and let it rest until the rhubarb is tender, 5 minutes. Let it cool completely before serving.

Unmold the mousse and assemble the dish: Dip the base of the mold into hot water and, using an offset spatula, gently coax it off the side of the mold, then flip it onto your serving plate and tap lightly to release. Top the yogurt mousse with the rhubarb and wildflower syrup, and serve.

Special Equipment

Hand mixer (optional)

6–8 molds (you can use mousse molds, ramekins, soufflé molds or decorative molds, or even make the mousse in a glass without unmolding)

Mousse

⅓ cup whole milk

6 tbsp honey

1 tbsp sugar

1¾ tsp gelatin

2 tsp cold water

1¾ cups buffalo yogurt (or plain, ideally around 5% M.F.)

1¼ cups 35% cream

Rhubarb

½ cup water

½ cup honey

½ cup sugar

4 stalks rhubarb, cut into 1-inch cubes (about 3 cups)

¼ cup edible wildflowers (optional, but we like a mix of marigold, chamomile, sweet clover and rose petals)

Nutty Chocolate Ganache Tart

MAKES 1 (12-INCH) TART **ALL SEASONS**

Special Equipment
12-inch removable-bottom tart pan
Food processor

Crust
3 cups mixed raw nuts (we like walnuts, blanched hazelnuts, pistachios and almonds)
7 tbsp brown sugar
¾ tsp kosher salt
5 tbsp unsalted butter, melted

Ganache
14 oz (400 g) bittersweet chocolate, chopped
2 cups 35% cream
7 tbsp unsalted butter, room temperature, cut into 1-inch cubes

Serving
Flaky sea salt

This tart is the dessert equivalent of the movie *The Notebook*. It seems basic on the surface, but if you look deeper, you'll find yourself an instant classic that's impossible to resist.

Preheat the oven and prepare the pan: Place a rack in the middle of the oven and preheat to 350°F. Lightly butter a 12-inch removable-bottom tart pan and line the bottom with a round of parchment paper.

Make the crust: Add the nuts to a food processor and pulse until finely chopped. Add the sugar and salt and pulse again to combine. Drizzle in the melted butter and pulse until the nuts begin to clump together and the mixture looks sandy. Transfer the mixture to the pan and use your hands to firmly and evenly press it into the bottom and up the sides of the pan (it doesn't need to come all the way up the sides). Bake the crust until it turns golden brown, about 15–20 minutes. Set aside to cool.

Make the ganache: Place the chocolate in a medium bowl. In a small pot, heat the cream until it's just beginning to simmer. Immediately pour it over the chocolate and let it sit, undisturbed, for 5 minutes. Add the butter and mix with a spatula until the mixture becomes smooth and glossy.

Assemble and chill: Pour the ganache into the crust and, using an offset spatula, smooth out any bubbles. Chill in the fridge, uncovered, until set, at least 1 hour.

Serve: Remove the tart from the pan and transfer to a plate. Sprinkle the top with flaky sea salt. Slice the tart into wedges with a hot knife for a clean cut. The tart can be made 1 day ahead and stored, covered, in the fridge.

Pistachio Cookies

MAKES 10–12 COOKIES   ALL SEASONS

These cookies are so addictive, they should probably be illegal. If you can resist eating them all in one sitting and wait a day or so, you'll be rewarded with an even chewier cookie with a deeper pistachio flavor. Our tip to make sure you don't eat them all right away? Simple. Lock two cookies in a double-bolted safe and give the key to someone you trust, telling them not to open it for 24 hours—no matter how much you beg.

Preheat the oven and prepare the baking sheet: Preheat the oven to 350°F and line a baking sheet with parchment paper. Place the icing sugar in a small bowl and set aside.

Mix the dry ingredients: In a food processor, place the pistachios, sugar and a generous pinch of salt and pulse until the nuts are coarsely ground with no large chunks left. Transfer to a medium bowl, add the almond flour and stir to combine.

Make the dough: In a small bowl, whisk together the egg whites, lemon zest, honey and vanilla. Add the egg white mixture to the dry ingredients and mix with your hands until the cookie dough starts sticking together and forming a mass, about 2 minutes

Roll the dough and bake the cookies: Divide the dough into golf-ball-size portions and roll each into a ball. Toss the balls in the icing sugar to fully coat them, then space them 2 inches apart on the prepared baking sheet. Using the palm of your hand, press lightly to flatten each ball.

Bake and cool: Bake the cookies until just starting to turn golden, 8–10 minutes. Remove from the oven and cool for at least 15 minutes on the baking sheet. The cookies will keep in an airtight container at room temperature for up to 1 week.

Special Equipment
Food processor

Pistachio Cookies
½ cup icing sugar, for dusting
1½ cups raw shelled pistachios
⅔ cup organic cane sugar
Pinch kosher salt
1 cup almond flour
2 egg whites
1 tsp finely grated lemon zest
1 tbsp honey
½ tsp vanilla

Concord Grape and Fennel Cake with Amaro Syrup

MAKES 1 (9-INCH) CAKE   SUMMER + AUTUMN

Special Equipment
9-inch cake pan

Cake
¾ cup all-purpose flour
¼ cup cornmeal
1 tsp baking powder
Pinch kosher salt
2 large eggs
¾ cup sugar
½ cup extra virgin olive oil
2 tbsp yogurt or sour cream
½ tbsp amaro (we like Amaro Euganeo for this recipe)
1 cup fresh or frozen concord grapes
1 tbsp organic sugar

Amaro Syrup
1 cup organic cane sugar
1 cup water
1 tsp fennel seeds
2 tbsp amaro
1½ cups fresh or frozen concord grapes

This recipe by Michelle Marek is the ultimate choose-your-own-adventure dessert because you can swap all the fruits, the fats and the types of flour and end up with an amazing cake every time. We dressed this one up in the style of a schiacciata con l'uva, a type of Tuscan flatbread made during harvest using wine grapes and fennel seeds.

Preheat the oven and prepare the pan: Preheat the oven to 350°F. Butter the bottom and sides of a 9-inch cake pan and dust the inside with sugar. Set aside.

Mix the dry ingredients: In a small bowl, whisk to combine the all-purpose flour, cornmeal, baking powder and salt. Set aside.

Whisk the wet ingredients: In a medium bowl, whisk the eggs, sugar and olive oil vigorously until light and creamy, about 30 seconds. Add the yogurt and amaro and whisk to combine.

Fold in the dry ingredients and fill the pan: Add the flour mixture to the wet ingredients and stir until no dry spots remain and the batter is just combined (be careful not to overmix). Pour the batter into the prepared pan and smooth out the top using a spatula. Distribute the concord grapes evenly around the surface of the cake and top with a light sprinkling of sugar.

Bake and cool: Bake the cake until a toothpick inserted into the center of the cake comes out clean, about 30–35 minutes. Allow the cake to cool a bit before removing it from the pan.

Make the amaro syrup: Meanwhile, in a medium pot, bring the sugar and water to a boil. In a small pan over medium heat, toast the fennel seeds until fragrant, 30 seconds. Add the fennel seeds to the boiling sugar water and turn off the heat. Add the amaro and stir to combine. Place the grapes in a large heatproof bowl, pour the syrup over the top, and let cool slightly. The syrup will keep for 1 month in the fridge.

Serve: Cut the cake into slices and serve warm, but not hot from the oven, with a drizzle of amaro syrup and syrupy grapes.

Apple and Quince Tart

MAKES 1 (10-INCH) TART   AUTUMN

Apple season is a big deal in Quebec. If you're going on a first date any time between mid-September and the end of October anywhere in the province, chances are you'll encounter an apple, whether it's on a restaurant menu or you're out apple picking. Janice's take on the classic apple pie uses quince, a fruit she has been obsessed with since she found a local producer outside of Montreal.

Make the pie dough: In a food processor, place the flour, butter and a pinch of salt, and pulse a few times until the butter gets broken down into small pieces. With the motor still running, slowly pour in the ice water until the dough begins to form a shaggy mass. Be careful not to overmix. Transfer the dough to a lightly floured surface and begin to very lightly knead it until the texture is somewhat homogeneous. Shape the dough into a ball, then flatten into a disk. Wrap it and chill in the fridge for at least 40 minutes. (This step can be done ahead of time, but make sure to wrap the dough very well to avoid drying.)

Prepare the quince puree: In a medium pot, bring the quince quarters, water, sugar, lemon zest and juice to a simmer. Continue cooking until the quinces have become tender enough to easily poke a fork through and have started to change color, about 1½ hours. Turn off the heat and let the quinces cool down in the cooking liquid. Once they are cool enough, remove them from the liquid, transfer to a blender or food processor and blend until very smooth. You should have enough quince puree to make a few pies. The puree can be made up to 1 week ahead of time and the leftovers can easily be frozen. We'd also recommend spreading some of the extra puree on your toasts in the morning; you won't regret it.

Make the filling: In a blender or food processor, place 1 cup quince puree, the brown sugar, eggs, butter, vanilla, vinegar and salt. Blend until smooth. This will make enough to fill two pies, but since quince are not in season for very long, we like to freeze the extra to make a fresh pie whenever the craving arises.

Special Equipment
Food processor
Blender

Pie Dough
3 cups all-purpose flour
1½ cups unsalted butter, very cold, cut into cubes
Pinch kosher salt
½ cup ice water

Quince Puree
2 quinces, peeled, cored and quartered
6 cups water
½ cup sugar
Zest and juice of 1 lemon

Quince Filling
1 cup brown sugar
2 large eggs
⅓ cup unsalted butter, room temperature
½ tbsp vanilla
½ tbsp white vinegar
½ tbsp kosher salt

Assembly
2 apples (we like crunchy varieties like Empire, Spartan or Granny Smith)
1 large egg yolk
2 tbsp 35% cream or whole milk
1 tsp granulated sugar
¾ tbsp icing sugar

(continued)

Temper the dough and preheat the oven: Remove the dough from the fridge to temper for 15 minutes before rolling it. Preheat the oven to 450°F.

Prepare the apples and the baking sheet: Cut and core the apples of your choice and slice them thinly. Line a baking sheet with parchment paper and set aside.

Roll out the dough and fill the tart: On a lightly floured surface, roll out the pie dough until you achieve a circle with about a 12-inch diameter and a thickness of ¼ inch. Carefully transfer the dough to the parchment-lined baking sheet. Spread about ¾ cup of the quince filling onto the dough, leaving a 3-inch border. Arrange the apple slices with some overlap (take your time with this step to make this as beautiful as possible). One portion at a time, fold back the edges of the dough toward the inside of the tart, pressing the dough gently to create little overlapping creases.

Brush the dough: In a small bowl, crack the egg, add the cream and beat lightly. Brush the outside of the tart with the egg and cream mixture. Sprinkle the entire tart with granulated sugar.

Bake the tart: Bake the tart at 450°F until the crust is golden brown, about 30 minutes. If the edges of the crust are not yet golden brown, reduce the heat to 425°F and bake for another 15 minutes. Transfer the tart to a rack and let it cool for 20 minutes. Sprinkle with icing sugar and serve.

THIS IS NOT THAT COFFEE

In life, you either have late nights or early mornings. Before we opened Elena, we decided that we were going to trade our after-hour spots for morning parks and lakes. With that shift in our schedule came an uptick in our coffee intake, and eventually we opened a secret-not-so-secret coffee shop and wine bar around back from Elena. You may know it as Elena around back, Coffee Pizza Wine, P.S., C.S., Club Social P.S. or C.S.P.S. We kind of lost track of how many different names people have given the place at this point. It also no longer feels like it's up to us to decide what it's called. It's a choose-your-own-adventure type of thing.

What is nonnegotiable, however, is how seriously we take our coffee. While a lot of people tend to think of coffee as a beverage that always tastes the same, we look at coffee the same way we look at wine. Think of commercial coffee as your conventional wine. That type of coffee is often a blend of beans that have been grown using a lot of chemicals and pesticides before going through heavy processing aimed at achieving specific flavor profiles that are popular in the market (like a bold, super-dark roast). It typically retains little to no trace of its natural aromas and flavor.

Single-origin coffee, which is what we've always served at Elena and now even roast ourselves under the label PS Coffee, is not that coffee. In many ways, it echoes the natural wine movement. Single-origin coffee acknowledges that a coffee is from a particular farm, co-op or producer located in a unique setting with very specific variables (crop variety, geography, elevation, temperature, soil, etc.) that impact the coffee's flavor and aromas. The coffee sourced by PS Coffee's sister company, Semilla Coffee—which holds multi-year relationships with grower communities in Rwanda, Honduras, Guatemala and Colombia—is grown without chemicals and gently processed. The same way most natural winemakers forgo organic certifications and appellation systems, most of our coffees are not certified organic for the simple reason that the certification can require a high fee for entry with minor increases in profits, and often remains unverified at the source. We roast our coffee gently to highlight the work of the producers we work with instead of masking its subtleties with a dark roast.

We take as much pleasure drinking coffee as we do drinking wine. There is just as much depth in a cup of coffee grown by our friend Esnaider Ortega-Gomez in Colombia (like notes of stone fruits, pineapple and bright citrus) than in any of the skin-contact natural wines you drink on the weekend. For us, coffee is not just something we pour in a cup (or five) each morning just to get on with our day. It is the result of a crop that is grown by farmers and coffee producers around the world. It is a product that changes with the seasons and vintages. Every sip tells the story of a place. And if you are interested in the stories behind where your food or your wine come from, then coffee should be no exception.

Chestnut Chocolate Cake

MAKES 1 (10-INCH) CAKE   **WINTER**

The original version of this cake was created by pastry chef Alexane Labonté and it may be the best chocolate cake we've ever had. Not only does the chestnut flour give it a deep, rich flavor, but the recipe is also deceptively simple.

Preheat the oven and prepare the cake pan: Preheat the oven to 400°F. Butter the bottom of a 10-inch cake pan and line it with parchment paper, pressing to remove air bubbles. Butter the parchment paper and the sides of the pan and set aside.

Brown the butter: Heat a medium pot over medium heat. Add the butter and cook until it becomes frothy and starts browning, about 4 minutes. Remove from the heat and let it cool slightly.

Make the crumble: In a stand mixer fitted with the paddle attachment, or in a food processor, place the chestnut flour, almond flour, sugar, butter cubes and salt. Pulse to combine until the mixture becomes crumbly but holds together when squeezed. Set aside.

Mix the batter and fill the pan: In a stand mixer fitted with the whisk attachment, or using a hand mixer in a large bowl, combine the icing sugar, almond flour, chestnut flour, cocoa powder, egg whites, salt and cooled brown butter. Mix until no dry spots remain and the batter is just combined. Pour the batter into the prepared pan and smooth out the top using a spatula. Top with the crumble.

Bake and cool: Place the cake in the oven, immediately turning the temperature down to 325°F. Bake the cake until the crumble is golden and a toothpick inserted into the center of the cake comes out clean, about 50 minutes. (It's OK if the cake jiggles a little; it will set as it cools down.) Allow the cake to cool before removing it from the pan, at least 30 minutes.

Whip the cream: In the bowl of a stand mixer fitted with the whisk attachment, or using a hand mixer, whip the cream and icing sugar until they form medium peaks. Serve with the cake.

Special Equipment
10-inch cake pan
Stand mixer or food processor and hand mixer

Cake
1½ cups unsalted butter
2½ cups icing sugar
1½ cups almond flour
½ cup chestnut flour
½ cup cocoa powder
10 egg whites (about 1¼ cups)
Pinch kosher salt

Crumble
½ cup chestnut flour
1 cup almond flour
½ cup sugar
½ cup unsalted butter, cold, cut into ½-inch cubes
¼ tsp kosher salt

Whipped Cream
¾ cup 35% cream
1 tbsp icing sugar

Polenta Orange Cake

MAKES 1 (9-INCH) CAKE   WINTER

Special Equipment
9-inch cake pan (springform if possible)

Cake
1 cup all-purpose flour

¼ cup polenta (coarse cornmeal)

⅓ cup almond flour

⅓ tsp baking powder

⅓ tsp baking soda

Pinch kosher salt

2 large eggs

1¼ cups sugar

¾ cup extra virgin olive oil

¾ cup whole milk

1 tbsp fresh lemon juice

1 tbsp orange juice

2 tbsp Confit Orange Puree (p. 269)

Zest of 1 lemon

Serving
½ cup Confit Orange Puree (p. 269)

⅓ cup amaro (we like Amaro Lucano for this recipe)

Polenta cake is one of the most understated and delicious Italian desserts there is. This version, developed by Michelle Marek, is no exception. It's the perfect cake to make at the peak of citrus season if you're looking to impart some sunshine to the darkest and coldest days of the year. If you happen to have any leftover orange amaro syrup, mix it with some sparkling water and pour it on ice for a super-low-ABV cocktail.

Preheat the oven and prepare the pan: Preheat the oven to 375°F. Butter a 9-inch cake pan and line it with parchment paper, pressing to remove air bubbles. Butter the parchment paper and set aside.

Mix the dry ingredients: In a small bowl, whisk to combine the all-purpose flour, polenta, almond flour, baking powder, baking soda and salt. Set aside.

Whisk the wet ingredients: In a large bowl, whisk the eggs, sugar and olive oil vigorously until light and creamy, about 30 seconds. Add the milk, lemon juice, orange juice, confit orange puree and lemon zest, and whisk to combine.

Fold in the dry ingredients and fill the pan: Add the flour mixture to the wet ingredients and stir until no dry spots remain and the batter is just combined. Be careful not to overmix. Pour the batter into the prepared pan.

Bake and cool: Place the cake in the oven and immediately reduce the heat to 350°F. Bake until a toothpick inserted into the center of the cake comes out clean, about 40–50 minutes. Allow the cake to cool a bit before removing it from the pan.

Make the orange amaro syrup: In a small bowl, whisk to combine ½ cup confit orange puree with the amaro.

Serve: Cut the cake into slices and serve with a drizzle of orange amaro syrup.

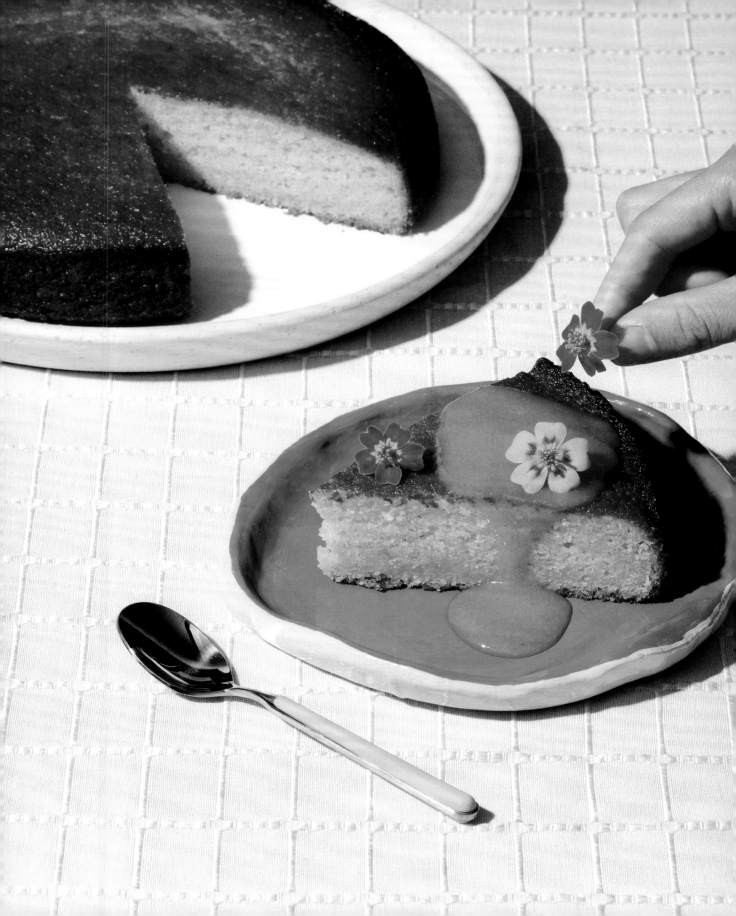

Babamisu

We thought it would be fun to combine two classic Italian desserts to create the most Italian treat—a tiramisu in which the lady fingers have been replaced with a Neapolitan baba brioche. And yes, it is as good and decadent as it sounds.

Make the yeast ball: In a small bowl, whisk to combine 2½ tbsp bread flour, the milk and the yeast. Form a small ball, then cover the bowl and place it in a warm spot. Leave it to rest for 30 minutes, during which the ball should double in size.

Beat the eggs: In a medium bowl, crack the eggs and beat lightly. Keep cold until ready to use.

Mix the baba dough: In a stand mixer fitted with the paddle attachment, combine the remaining bread flour, sugar, salt and yeast ball. Mix on medium speed, adding the beaten eggs gradually. (The dough should seem fairly wet at this point, almost like batter.) Increase the speed and mix for 7–10 minutes. Rest the dough for 2 minutes, then mix for another 7–10 minutes, scraping down the bowl with a spatula from time to time. The mixture should start looking more like dough, becoming stretchier, shinier and stickier, as it pulls away from the sides of the bowl.

After about a total of 15–20 minutes of mixing and with the mixer still running, start adding the butter in small knobs, allowing it to fully incorporate into the dough before adding the next knob. Continue mixing until all the butter has been blended in, about 10 minutes. Remove the bowl from the mixer, cover and place in a warm spot. Leave the dough there for 3–4 hours, during which it should triple in volume.

Prepare the mascarpone cream: In a small pot, bring the milk to a simmer. Meanwhile, whisk to combine the sugar, salt, cornstarch, egg, egg yolks and vanilla in a medium bowl. While continuing to whisk, add half of the warm milk in a steady stream to the egg mixture to temper it. Gradually add the remaining milk, a few tablespoons at a time, into the egg mixture, whisking after each

Special Equipment
Stand mixer
12 mini fluted molds (or a 12-cup muffin pan) or 1 large Bundt pan

Baba
2⅓ cups bread flour, divided
1 tbsp whole milk
¾ tsp instant dry yeast
6 large eggs
⅓ cup sugar
¼ tsp kosher salt
½ cup unsalted butter, room temperature

Mascarpone Cream
1 cup whole milk
¼ cup sugar
Pinch kosher salt
2 tbsp cornstarch
1 large egg
2 large egg yolks
¼ tsp vanilla
1½ cups Mascarpone (p. 274)
1 cup 35% cream

Coffee Syrup
1 cup hot brewed filter coffee
½ cup water
¾ cup sugar
¼ cup coffee liqueur or coffee amaro

Assembly
Cocoa nibs
Cocoa powder (optional)

(continued)

addition. When all the ingredients are combined, transfer everything back to the pot and cook on medium heat until the mixture has thickened and become smooth, about 5–10 minutes. Transfer it to a container, cover to avoid a film forming and place in the fridge to cool down completely.

Finish making the mascarpone cream: Once the pastry cream has cooled completely, add it to a mixing bowl with the mascarpone. Whisk together until it is smooth and even. In a separate bowl, whisk the cream until stiff peaks form. Fold the whipped cream into the mascarpone mixture until fully combined. Cover and chill until ready to use.

Prepare and fill the molds or pan: When the dough has tripled in volume, butter 12 mini fluted molds or a large Bundt pan and lightly dust with flour. Punch down the dough with your hands to make it a bit more compact, then let it rest for a few minutes. If you are making 12 mini babas, use a spoon to portion the dough (roughly 2 oz/56 g each) and add it to the molds. Wet your fingers and then gently pat the top of each mound of dough to even out the surface. If you are making one large baba, simply add the dough to the Bundt pan. Cover the filled pan with a damp towel and place it in a warm spot. Let the dough rest and proof for 40 minutes.

Bake and cool: Preheat the oven to 350°F. Bake until the dough turns golden brown, about 15–25 minutes. Remove from the oven and cool in the pan for at least 10 minutes before unmolding. Transfer to a rack to cool down completely. The baba(s) can be stored in an airtight container in the fridge for up to 1 week or in the freezer for several months.

Make the coffee syrup: In a small pot, bring the hot coffee, water and sugar to a boil, whisking until the sugar has completely dissolved. Turn off the heat and add the liqueur or amaro. Transfer to a large bowl and set aside.

Assemble the dish: In a large bowl, place the baba(s) in the coffee syrup, spooning the syrup over them and flipping them so they become evenly soaked. This should take about 15 minutes for small babas and 25 minutes for one large baba. Place the baba(s) on a rack to cool down. Serve the baba(s) with a generous dollop of the mascarpone cream, top with cocoa nibs and dust liberally with cocoa powder (optional).

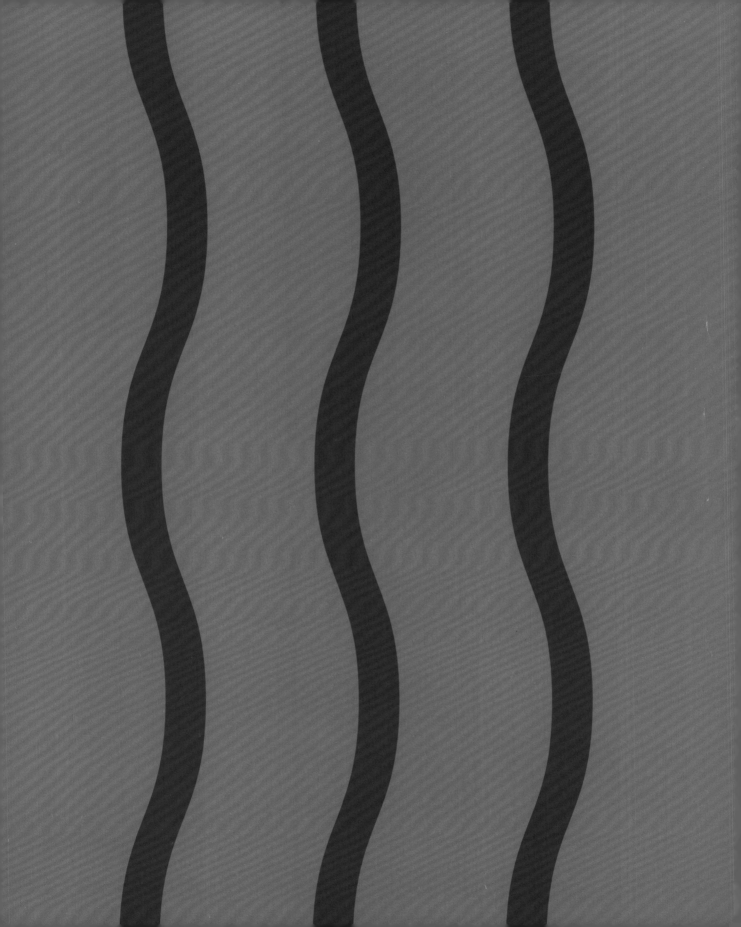

We use these recipes throughout the book to add dimension and depth to our dishes. Think of them as the foundation of your adventure with *Salad Pizza Wine*. In this chapter, we will show you our basic techniques for toasting nuts, what to do with stale bread and how to preserve vibrant summer vegetables. We will even teach you how to make your own fresh cheese (it's a lot easier than you think). You will find plenty of ways to make the most of our go-to recipes, well beyond the pages of this book.

TEXTURE STATION

Toasted Breadcrumbs

MAKES ABOUT 2 CUPS

We don't have many rules in the kitchen (we usually want people to follow their instincts and cook to their liking), but this one is basically canon at this point: never throw away bread! There are so many uses for stale bread or bread ends, and these toasted breadcrumbs are a great example. We like to always have a batch handy to add texture and flavor to pasta, salads and vegetable dishes.

Toast the bread: Preheat the oven to 250°F. Trim off any thick part of the crust and cut the bread into 1-inch cubes. Spread the cubes on a baking sheet in a single layer and bake until completely dry, but not browned, about 1 hour. Don't worry, it's OK if the pieces take on a tiny bit of color. Cool fully, then place in a food processor and pulse into crumbs. You want the crumbs to be roughly the same size—small, but not powdery.

Cook the breadcrumbs: Line a baking sheet with paper towel. In a large frying pan, heat 4 tbsp olive oil over medium heat. Add the breadcrumbs and start stirring with a wooden spoon or heat-proof spatula so that they toast gradually without burning. Lower the heat if needed. When they've taken on a bit of color, add the chopped parsley and chilies. Once the crumbs have reached a nice golden-brown color, move them to the side of the pan. Add 1 tsp olive oil and, using a Microplane, finely grate the garlic directly into the pan. Stir slowly to evenly incorporate the garlic into the breadcrumbs. Remove from the heat and add the lemon zest and a generous pinch of salt. Spread evenly onto the paper towel–lined baking sheet to absorb the excess oil. Store the breadcrumbs in an airtight container at room temperature for up to 3 days.

Special Equipment
Food processor

½ loaf country or sourdough bread (about 11 oz/340 g)
4 tbsp + 1 tsp extra virgin olive oil, divided
2 tbsp finely chopped fresh parsley
Finely chopped fresh chili, to your liking
1–2 cloves garlic
Finely grated zest of 1 lemon
Kosher salt

Seasoned Breadcrumbs

MAKES ABOUT 2 CUPS

Special Equipment
Food processor

½ loaf sourdough bread (about 11 oz/340 g)
½ cup grated parmesan
½ tbsp garlic powder
¾ tsp mustard powder
¾ tsp kosher salt
¼ tsp freshly ground black pepper

This is a recipe you will use time and again. You can use our seasoned breadcrumbs to bread anything from eggplant (p. 206) and chicken (p. 219) to fish, veal Milanese or even tofu. And the great thing about it is that you can easily adapt it to your taste, such as making it spicier by adding a few teaspoons of dried chili flakes.

Toast the bread: Preheat the oven to 250°F. Trim off any thick part of the crust and cut the bread into 1-inch cubes. Spread the cubes on a baking sheet in a single layer and bake until completely dry, but not browned, about 1 hour. Don't worry, it's OK if the pieces take on a tiny bit of color. Cool fully, then place in a food processor and pulse into crumbs. You want the crumbs to be roughly the same size—small, but not powdery.

Add the seasoning: In a medium bowl, toss to combine the pulsed breadcrumbs, parmesan, garlic powder, mustard powder, salt and pepper. Store in an airtight container at room temperature for up to 3 days.

Garlic Croutons

MAKES ABOUT 3 CUPS, DEPENDING ON THE
SIZE OF YOUR LOAF

½ loaf country or sourdough bread (about 11 oz/340 g)
½ cup extra virgin olive oil
½ tsp kosher salt
1 clove garlic

Even though this recipe makes about 3 cups of croutons, we highly recommend doubling it right away because you're going to end up snacking on half of them before they're even done cooking (it's called taste testing, look it up). If you plan on adding the croutons to your salad straight out of the oven, we recommend cooking them three-quarters of the way through so that they're crispy on the outside and tender on the inside.

Bake the bread: Preheat the oven to 400°F. Cut the bread into 1-inch-thick slices. Place the slices on a baking sheet in a single layer and douse them with the olive oil until both sides are fairly saturated. Sprinkle both sides with the salt. Bake for 8–10 minutes, until the bread is just starting to brown, turning each slice halfway through. Remove from the oven and cool slightly.

Make the croutons: Cut the garlic clove in half and rub it on both sides of each slice of bread to impart a bit of flavor. Cut the slices into 1-inch cubes. The croutons can be made 1 day ahead and stored in an airtight container.

Toasted and Fried Nuts and Seeds

While we like to toast most of our nuts and seeds in the oven, we prefer to pan-fry smaller varieties like pine nuts and sunflower seeds. It's easier to gauge the exact moment when they're done, plus we're left with delicious nut-infused oil, which can be strained and reused later to give a nutty kick to a vinaigrette. Buy the best quality nuts you can afford in small quantities and store them in the freezer, where they'll remain fresh longer (nuts are packed with natural oils that can go rancid). Only roast what you'll need for the recipe (don't forget to account for snacking) to ensure ultimate freshness.

Toasting method: Preheat the oven to 300°F. Place the nuts or seeds on a baking sheet and toast until the color has changed slightly and you can start smelling the nuttiness. The exact baking time will depend on the type and size of the nuts. (Pistachios will toast quickly, for example, while hazelnuts will require more time.) Taste them to make sure, or cut them to look inside—a good way to tell if they're ready is if the texture inside is even throughout.

Pan-frying method: Line a baking sheet with paper towel and set up a fine-mesh strainer over a metal bowl. In a small pot over medium heat, heat enough oil to cover the nuts or seeds. Add the nuts or seeds and cook slowly, stirring gently to ensure even cooking. Lower the heat if necessary to avoid burning. Once you notice that the color has changed and can smell the nuttiness, quickly remove from the heat. Strain the oil through the fine-mesh strainer and save it for later use or discard. Spread the nuts evenly onto the paper towel–lined baking sheet to absorb the excess oil and prevent further cooking.

Hoagie Spice Mix

MAKES 2½ CUPS

½ cup raw sesame seeds
½ cup raw poppy seeds
¼ cup dried oregano
2 tbsp flaky sea salt
1 tbsp freshly ground black pepper
¼ cup onion powder

This is what we use to top our hoagie buns, but it can also be used to add a bit of texture to your favorite salad.

Make the spice mix: Place all the ingredients in a medium bowl and toss to mix. Store in a spice jar with large holes for easy sprinkling.

SAUCES, DRESSINGS + OTHER FRIENDS

Tomato Sauce

MAKES 7½ CUPS

This is a very versatile tomato sauce that we use throughout the book. It's what we cook our Meatballs (p. 185) and dip our Suppli (p. 151) in. It's also a simple, well-balanced tomato sauce to have in your arsenal when you want to make pasta or a lasagna. Using good-quality canned tomatoes (read about our preferences on p. 11) will go a long way toward making this simple tomato sauce really special, as does cooking it very slowly and gently. We recommend doubling or tripling the recipe and freezing any leftovers so that you always have some sauce handy.

Cook the vegetables: In a large pot, heat the olive oil over medium-low heat. Once the oil is hot, add the onions, garlic and chili flakes and slowly cook until translucent, making sure they don't brown, about 5 minutes. If the oil gets too hot, pull the pan off the heat for a few moments and lower the heat before resuming cooking. Add the tomatoes and cook slowly for 2 hours, stirring every so often to avoid sticking.

Make the sauce: If you have a food mill, now is the perfect time to use it. Otherwise, attack the big chunks with an immersion blender or a potato masher—just avoid using a regular blender because it will emulsify the sauce. The sauce will keep for a week in the fridge or a few months in the freezer.

Special Equipment

Food mill, immersion blender or potato masher

1 cup extra virgin olive oil
3 onions, diced
6 large cloves garlic, thinly sliced
¼ tsp dried chili flakes
3 (28 oz/796 ml) cans peeled whole tomatoes

Chris's Crispy Chili Oil

MAKES 2 CUPS

Special Equipment

Frying thermometer

1¾ cups vegetable oil or other neutral oil

8 cloves garlic

1 large shallot, peeled and quartered

1 tsp black peppercorns

1 tsp coriander seeds

1 tsp fennel seeds

2 bay leaves, lightly crushed

1 tbsp kosher salt

¼ cup crushed dried Espelette peppers or dried chili flakes

1½ tbsp crushed cayenne peppers

This chili oil packs a super-flavorful, toasted and warm heat that's not outrageously spicy. At the restaurant, we drizzle it on our pizza, but you can also use it on pasta dishes like our Corn Agnolotti (p. 139).

Confit the alliums: Attach a frying thermometer to the side of a small pot. Add the oil, garlic, shallots, peppercorns, coriander seeds, fennel seeds and bay leaves, and cook over low heat until the temperature reaches somewhere between 200°F and 225°F. Continue cooking, maintaining the temperature, for at least 1 hour and up to 2 hours. (Cooking the garlic and shallots in oil at a low temperature for a couple of hours results in perfect confit alliums, which helps the chili oil stay fresher longer.)

Make the chili oil: In a heatproof bowl, combine the salt, crushed Espelette peppers and crushed cayenne peppers. Using a strainer, pour the hot oil mixture in the bowl, stirring immediately to make sure the chilies and salt get fully incorporated into the oil. Let the chili oil cool down to room temperature. Transfer to a clean mason jar and keep in the fridge for up to 6 months.

Spicy Honey

MAKES 1 CUP

The spicy honey we sell at the restaurant is made with honey that's produced by our friends Anicet Desrochers and Anne-Virginie Schmidt at Les Miels d'Anicet, a magical bee farm just a few hours north of Montreal. They make a few different types of honey throughout the year (and tons of other amazing honey-derived products), with some of the most unique flavor profiles, including a mild and herbaceous spring nectar, a minty-fresh linden summer honey and a rustic buckwheat honey with caramelized, barnlike aromas. For this recipe, we gently infuse the honey with Espelette peppers at a relatively low heat (never reaching above 105°F) to avoid affecting its natural texture. It feels a bit like making a cup of tea in a way. You obviously don't have to use Miels d'Anicet to make this, but try to find organic honey from a producer in your area—you'll taste the difference right away.

2 tsp ground Espelette pepper or chili of your choice

½ tsp flaky sea salt

1 cup good-quality unpasteurized honey

Make the spicy honey: In a small pot over medium-high heat, bring to a boil enough water to cover an 8 oz (250 ml) jar. In a small bowl, whisk together the ground Espelette pepper, salt and 1½ tbsp water. In another small pot (not the one with the boiling water), combine the honey and the salty Espelette pepper water. Cook over low heat until the honey is warm and fluid, below 105°F, about 1–2 minutes.

Pack the spicy honey: Pour the warm honey directly into a clean 8 oz (250 ml) mason jar and close it tightly. Take the boiling water off the heat and gently submerge the closed mason jar into the water. Allow it to steep until the water has completely cooled down. The honey will keep in this jar at room temperature for several months.

Bomba

MAKES 3 CUPS

Special Equipment
Food processor

Pepper base
2 large sweet red peppers, seeded and roughly chopped (about 3 cups)

12–15 spicy peppers, seeded and roughly chopped (about 2½ cups)

1½ tbsp kosher salt

2 tbsp sugar

⅓ cup red wine vinegar

Duxelles
¼ cup coarsely chopped shallots

½ cup coarsely chopped eggplant

¼ cup coarsely chopped button mushrooms

1 clove garlic, cut in half

¾ cup extra virgin olive oil, divided

1 tsp kosher salt

½ tsp ground coriander

½ tsp ground fennel

2 tsp tomato paste

This is our go-to spicy condiment. Toss it in with roasted brussels sprouts for a quick side dish, fold it into tomato sauce to turn it into an arrabiata sauce or simply use it to dip your bread. For the peppers, try a mix of sweet varieties like red bell, Carmen, Corno di Toro and chocolate, and hot peppers such as red long hot, red jalapeno, Espelette, Cherry Bomb and cayenne.

Prepare and brine the peppers: In a food processor, combine the sweet peppers and spicy peppers and pulse for 15 seconds, until the peppers turn into a paste. Transfer to a nonreactive bowl. Add the salt, sugar and vinegar and stir to combine. Cover loosely and leave on the counter for 12 hours or overnight to ferment.

Make the mushroom duxelles: In a food processor, combine the shallots, eggplant, mushrooms and garlic and pulse until finely chopped, about 10–15 seconds. In a small pot, heat ½ cup olive oil over medium-low heat. Stir in the shallot-eggplant mixture, salt, coriander and fennel. Sweat the vegetables, stirring often, for 15 minutes. Add the tomato paste and continue cooking until the oil separates from the vegetable mixture and the puree turns a nice chocolate brown, 10 minutes. Remove from the heat, add the remaining ¼ cup oil and let it cool.

Make the bomba: Stir the duxelles into the fermented pepper base, adjust seasoning to taste and transfer to a mason jar. This will keep in the fridge for up to 1 month.

Hoagie Mayonnaise

MAKES 1 CUP

1 large egg yolk
½ tsp Dijon mustard
⅓ tbsp red wine vinegar
⅓ tsp kosher salt
1 cup canola oil
1 tsp water

Every home cook should know how to make their own mayonnaise, because it's 100 times better than anything you will ever buy and it's really easy to make. Our version is super tangy. That's just how we roll. If you're making a double batch, you can use the leftover egg whites to make our Pistachio Cookies (p. 231).

Make the mayonnaise: In a medium bowl, whisk together the egg yolk, mustard, vinegar and salt. Gradually add the canola oil, whisking continuously to help the mayonnaise emulsify. When you're done adding all the oil, the mayonnaise should feel quite thick. Add 1 tsp water to loosen it up. Taste and adjust the seasoning with salt. The mayonnaise will keep for up to 2 weeks in the fridge.

Sage Mayonnaise

MAKES 1 CUP

Special Equipment
Blender

10 leaves fresh sage (a handful)
1 cup canola oil, divided

Now that you know how to make mayonnaise, you can build on those skills by adding some aromatics. This is the sage version we use for the Porchetta and Sage hoagie (p. 215), but you can choose your own adventure and replace the sage with other herbs like basil, tarragon, parsley or saffron.

Make the sage oil: In a small pot, heat the sage and ¼ cup canola oil over medium heat. Cook until the sage turns deep green and the oil becomes very fragrant, about 3–5 minutes. Turn off the heat. Add ¾ cup canola oil to the pot and let it cool down. Transfer the oil to a blender and pulse until the sage has broken down.

Make the mayonnaise: Use the sage oil to replace the canola oil and follow the instructions for the Hoagie Mayonnaise recipe (to the left). The mayonnaise will keep for up to 2 weeks in the fridge.

Hoagie Mustard

MAKES 2½ CUPS

Special Equipment
Blender or immersion blender

1 cup mustard seeds
1 tsp smoked paprika (we like La Dalia)
1½ tsp turmeric powder
2 tbsp kosher salt
2 tsp sugar
1 tsp black peppercorns
1 tsp garlic powder
1¾ cups apple cider vinegar
1 cup water

In Quebec, we typically call yellow mustard "baseball mustard," and like most places in the world, that kind of mustard is typically found in a yellow plastic bottle that gets squeezed on a hot dog or a corn dog. But here's the thing: it's actually pretty easy (and really baller, pun intended) to serve your friends a sandwich with mustard you made yourself.

Soak the ingredients: In a container with a lid, combine the mustard seeds, paprika, turmeric, salt, sugar, peppercorns, garlic powder and apple cider vinegar. Seal the container with its lid and soak at room temperature for at least 12 hours and up to 1 week (the longer it soaks, the softer the mustard seeds will become).

Cook the mustard: Once the soaking is done, pour the vinegar mixture in a heavy-bottomed pot and add the water. Place the lid slightly askew and cook on low, stirring often to prevent any sticking and burning, until the mustard seeds have softened, up to 1½ hours depending on how long the mixture soaked beforehand. Turn off the heat and let it cool down slightly.

Blend the mustard: Transfer the cooled-down mixture to a blender, or use an immersion blender, and pulse until homogeneous. (You want the mustard to be somewhat smooth while keeping some texture.) As it continues to cool down, you'll see if you need to adjust the texture and seasoning with more salt, water, sugar or vinegar. The hoagie mustard will keep in the fridge for up to 6 months.

Pine Nut Puree

Special Equipment
Blender

1 cup pan-fried pine nuts and their cooking oil (follow the method on p. 253 using 5 tbsp neutral oil), cooled to room temperature
⅓ cup cold water
1 tsp sugar
¾ tsp kosher salt
2 tbsp red wine vinegar

This sauce is delicious in our radish salad (p. 23), as a nice wintery dip alternative to our Pinzimonio (p. 25) or dolloped on a roasted vegetable platter. You can also thin it out with some oil or water and dress a green salad with it.

Make the pine nut puree: In a blender, place the cooled pan-fried pine nuts and their cooking oil and blend until smooth. With the motor running, gradually add the cold water, followed by the sugar, salt and vinegar. Taste and adjust the seasoning with more salt if needed. If you notice your puree is starting to split, it means it's probably too warm. Simply remove it from the blender and chill before whisking it back together. The pine nut puree will keep in the fridge for up to 1 week.

Salsa Verde

⅓ cup extra virgin olive oil
4 anchovy fillets, finely chopped
2 tbsp fresh lemon juice
1 clove garlic, finely chopped or Microplaned
4 tbsp diced Pickled Shallots (p. 280)
1 cup roughly chopped fresh mint leaves
1 cup roughly chopped fresh parsley leaves
½ cup roughly chopped fresh chives
¼ tsp dried chili flakes or ½ fresh red chili, minced
⅛ tsp freshly ground black pepper

Every home cook should have a simple salsa verde recipe up their sleeve. This one comes together in only a few minutes and is a great addition to pretty much anything. Mix it into a grain salad, dollop a spoonful on a seared steak or toss it with raw zucchini ribbons and roasted peppers (p. 41).

Make the salsa verde: In a medium bowl, place the olive oil, anchovies, lemon juice, garlic, pickled shallots, chopped mint, parsley, chives, chili flakes and black pepper. Stir to combine. The salsa verde will keep for up to 1 week in the fridge.

Dante Vinegar

MAKES ½ CUP

Special Equipment
Blender (optional)

½ cup white wine vinegar
1½ cloves garlic, minced
2¼ tsp dried oregano
2¼ tsp garlic powder
¾ tsp kosher salt
½ tsp freshly ground black pepper

We like to make a big batch of this spiced vinegar because it lasts a really long time, and it is super versatile. On its own, it makes for a great marinade for chicken (Dante Chicken Thighs, p. 181), and when you mix it with olive oil, it becomes a great vinaigrette (Dante Salad, p. 30).

Make the vinegar: Whisk all the ingredients together in a bowl or blitz in a blender until smooth. The Dante vinegar will keep in the fridge indefinitely.

Tonnato

MAKES 2 CUPS

Special Equipment
Blender

10 oil-packed anchovy fillets, drained
1 clove garlic
2 tbsp Dijon mustard
2 tbsp fresh lemon juice
5 large egg yolks
5 tbsp extra virgin olive oil, divided
1 tbsp white wine, divided
2 (5.6 oz/160 g) cans oil-packed tuna, drained
3 tsp capers, rinsed and drained
½ tsp kosher salt
¼ tsp freshly ground black pepper

I know we said we don't really have rules in the kitchen, so let's call this one a tip. Never buy water-packed tuna! It's not nearly as good as the oil-packed versions, so you're basically doing yourself a disservice by doing that. Tonnato is a classic Italian condiment that is often dumbed down to being tuna mayonnaise, but it's so much more than that. Tonnato is packed with flavors that can spruce up a lot of dishes: use it as a dip for vegetables, spread it on warm bread, serve it with sliced veal for a classic vitello tonnato or make Tomato Tonnato (p. 34).

Make the tonnato: In a blender, combine the anchovies, garlic, mustard, lemon juice, egg yolks, half of the olive oil and half of the white wine. Pulse until smooth. Add the tuna, capers, salt, pepper and remaining olive oil and white wine. Blend until smooth. Taste and adjust the seasoning with more lemon juice, salt and pepper. The tonnato will keep in the fridge for up to 1 week.

Pistachio Pesto

MAKES 2 CUPS

Special Equipment
Food processor

1 cup lightly toasted pistachios (see p. 253)
2 cups packed arugula
1¼ cups roughly chopped fresh parsley leaves
1 cup roughly chopped fresh chives
Zest of 1 lemon
⅔ cup extra virgin olive oil, divided
Kosher salt
Freshly ground black pepper

We use this on two of our pizzas, but this pesto is delicious tossed in pasta or with roasted vegetables like green beans. If you don't have arugula on hand, feel free to replace it with parsley.

Make the condiment: Put the pistachios in a food processor and process until roughly chopped. Add the arugula, parsley, chives, lemon zest and half of the olive oil and pulse until the mixture is roughly blended but still slightly coarse. Scrape the mixture from the food processor into a bowl and stir in the rest of the olive oil. Season with salt and pepper to taste. Store in the fridge for up to 5 days.

Oven-Dried Cherry Tomatoes

MAKES 3 CUPS

2 lb (900 g) cherry tomatoes, cut in half
1 tbsp picked fresh rosemary leaves
1 tbsp picked fresh thyme leaves
½ tsp kosher salt
1 tbsp extra virgin olive oil

If you're anything like us, there's a chance you tend to go a bit overboard when it comes to buying cherry tomatoes in the peak of summer. This recipe is a great way to use the tomatoes you haven't had time to eat when they're starting to get soft. We love these slow-roasted tomatoes on toast, pizza or fish or tossed in a simple pasta dish with nice olive oil and grated parmesan. They're also the base for our Olive Tapenade (p. 268).

Preheat the oven and prepare the ingredients: Preheat the oven to 350°F and line a baking sheet with parchment paper. In a large bowl, toss to combine the cut tomatoes, rosemary, thyme, salt and olive oil.

Cook the tomatoes: Arrange the tomatoes cut side up on the baking sheet. Cook in the oven for 15 minutes. Reduce the heat down to 250°F and continue cooking until the tomatoes have lost over half of their juices and are slightly caramelized, about 45 minutes. Serve warm with the Stuffed Roasted Fish (p. 179) or cool down to make the Olive Tapenade (p. 268).

Peach Mostarda

MAKES 3 CUPS

Special Equipment
Food processor

4 medium peaches, pitted and quartered

1 cup + 2 tbsp sugar

Finely grated zest of 1 lemon

1 cup golden raisins or another dry fruit of your choice, cut into smaller pieces

2 tbsp white wine, marsala or brandy

1 tsp kosher salt

3 tbsp freshly ground mustard seeds

3 tbsp whole mustard seeds

2 tbsp white wine vinegar

2 tbsp extra virgin olive oil

Although this recipe calls for peaches, you can use these directions to make mostarda with a variety of fruits, like pears, plums and cherries. We use the peach version to accompany our porchetta (p. 183), but it is also delicious with a simple pork chop or with a sharp cheddar as part of a cheese platter.

Marinate the peaches: Place the peach quarters and the sugar in a food processor and pulse a few times to slightly break up the pieces. Transfer to a bowl and add the lemon zest, raisins, wine and salt. Toss to combine. Pack into a clean mason jar and let it rest at room temperature for at least 12 hours or overnight.

Finish the mostarda: Transfer the marinated peaches to a bowl and add the freshly ground mustard seeds, whole mustard seeds, white wine vinegar and olive oil. Stir well to combine. Enjoy right away atop a slice of porchetta (p. 183) or store in a clean mason jar in the fridge for up to 6 months. As it ages, the mustardy kick will soften, the flavors will become much more complex and the texture should thicken slightly because the mustard seeds will slowly absorb the liquid.

Romesco Sauce

MAKES 1½ CUPS

Even if it's in the name, romesco sauce unfortunately did not originate from Rome (our favorite city). The sauce actually comes from the town of Tarragona, Spain. But because the town used to be part of the Roman empire, it feels Roman enough for us to want to spread it on anything, from homemade fritters and thick slices of crusty bread with anchovies to delicate pieces of steamed white fish and roasted meats.

Roast the vegetables: Preheat the oven to 450°F and line a baking sheet with parchment paper. Remove the core of the tomato and cut out an x at the bottom. On the baking sheet, place the tomato x side up, the red bell pepper cut side down and the chili whole. Sprinkle the vegetables with 1 tbsp olive oil and a generous pinch of salt. Bake until the tomato and the peppers have softened and their skins look wilted, puckered and slightly blackened, about 25 minutes.

Peel and seed the vegetables: Let the tomato cool on the baking sheet while you place the peppers inside a covered container to cool and steam for 30 minutes. Once the peppers and tomato are cool enough to handle, remove the skins. Peel the tomato, cut it along the equator and open it up over a colander to let the seeds and juices drip out.

Make garlic oil: In the meantime, in a small saucepan, heat ½ cup olive oil over medium heat. Add the grated garlic cloves and cook until fragrant, 1 minute. Set aside to cool.

Blend the romesco sauce: In a food processor, pulse the pine nuts and hazelnuts until finely chopped, but not pasty. Add the roasted peppers and tomato and process until just combined. Pour in the white balsamic vinegar and cooled garlic oil. Pulse. Taste and adjust the seasoning with salt and pepper. Use immediately or transfer to an airtight container and store in the fridge for up to 1 week.

Special Equipment
Food processor

1 large tomato

1 red bell pepper, top cut and core removed

1 fresh chili (such as serrano)

1 tbsp + ½ cup extra virgin olive oil, divided

Kosher salt

3 cloves garlic, grated

½ cup pan-fried pine nuts (see p. 253)

½ cup toasted hazelnuts (see p. 253)

2 tbsp white balsamic vinegar

Freshly ground black pepper

Olive Tapenade

MAKES 1¾ CUPS

Special Equipment
Food processor

1 cup Oven-Dried Cherry Tomatoes (p. 265) or store-bought sundried tomatoes in oil
1 cup pitted black olives (we like Taggiasca or kalamata)
½ cup extra virgin olive oil
1 clove garlic
Finely grated zest of 1 lemon
Pinch dried chili flakes

When she's too busy to sit down and eat a real meal, one of Janice's go-to snacks is to eat cucumbers dipped in this olive tapenade. It's a great, super-easy-to-make recipe to have up your sleeve. You can spread it on a vegetarian sandwich (Dr. Lyle, p. 211) or use it to top a meat or fish dish. Keep some around at all times and you won't have a problem finding ways to use it.

Make the tapenade: Place all the ingredients in a food processor and pulse until well chopped and textured, but not completely pureed. The tapenade will keep in the fridge for up to 1 week.

Simple Syrup

MAKES 1 CUP

1 cup granulated sugar
1 cup water

Simple is in the name for a reason. Maybe this shouldn't be considered a recipe, but we reference it a few times in this book, so we had to have it here. Plus, we think everyone should know how to make it, so here we are.

Make the simple syrup: In a small saucepan, heat the sugar and water over medium heat, whisking until the sugar has completely dissolved. Turn off the heat and let it cool. Transfer to a mason jar and store in the fridge for up to 1 month.

Confit Orange Puree

MAKES 1 CUP

Mix this puree with wine vinegar and oil to create a zesty salad dressing (Radicchio and Citrus Salad with Black Olives, p. 61) or whisk in some amaro to make a sweet and slightly boozy syrup to drizzle over a simple cake like our Polenta Orange Cake (p. 240). You can use this recipe to confit orange peels, which you can use to garnish a variety of desserts or serve with fresh ricotta in a cannoli.

Boil the orange peels: Using a kitchen peeler, remove the skin of each orange in wide strips (don't worry if you remove some of the pith). In a small pot, put the peels and enough water to cover them (about 3 cups). Bring to a boil, then immediately drain out the water using a fine-mesh strainer and rinse the peels. Transfer the peels back to the pot with more fresh water and repeat this process two more times. Drain the peels after the third boil and return to the empty pot.

Confit the orange: Juice the peeled oranges and add ½ cup of the juice to the pot of boiled peels along with ½ cup water and the sugar. Cook the orange mixture over medium heat, stirring every so often, until the peels are tender and shiny and the liquid has reduced by half and turned into a syrup, about 20 minutes. Remove from the heat and let it cool for a few minutes.

Blend the confit oranges: Transfer the confit orange peels and their syrup to a blender and pulse until smooth. The confit orange puree will keep in the fridge for several months.

Special Equipment
Blender

3 oranges
½ cup water
1 cup sugar

Creamy Polenta, p. 276

DAIRY THINGS

Stracciatella

MAKES 3 CUPS

Traditional Italian stracciatella is made from pulled mozzarella di bufala curds mixed with heavy cream. But because we are from Quebec—a province whose culinary culture is essentially built on poutine—we make ours with the same fresh cheese curds you find at the local casse-croûte, grocery store or even gas station. To achieve the proper consistency of this fresh-curd stracciatella cheese, it is important to use room-temperature, never-refrigerated cheese curds. Refrigerating changes the curds' texture and makes them hard to use for stracciatella. If you don't live somewhere where fresh cheese curds are available to you, you can call your local cheese shop and ask if they have any.

Heat the water: Bring the water to a boil and keep it boiling for 30 minutes to dechlorinate it. Lower the heat and use a thermometer to measure and maintain a temperature of 191°F.

Cool the cream: Fill a large bowl with ice. Grab a medium bowl that fits over your large bowl and pour in the cream. Set it over the ice bowl to keep the cream cold.

Make the stracciatella: In a large mixing bowl, combine the cheese curds and salt and use your hands to break up the curds into even 1-inch cubes. Toss to combine.

Pour 4 cups of 191°F water (make sure you check the temperature before) over the salted cheese curds and, using a wooden spoon, stir vigorously until the curds begin to soften, about 1 minute. Drain and discard about three-quarters of the water.

(continued)

Special Equipment
Instant-read thermometer

20 cups water
2 cups 35% cream
1 lb (450 g) fresh cheddar cheese curds (never refrigerated)
2¾ tbsp fine sea salt

Add 6 more cups of 191°F water. Stir back and forth in a semicircular motion until the curds start to clump together. Once they've formed a mass, use tongs to lift it up and out of the water to stretch it, then bring it back down into the water. If the cheese starts breaking instead of stretching, dump out some of the water and replace it with more 191°F water. Repeat this motion until the lumps are gone and the mass has coalesced and looks smooth and shiny, about 10 times. Drain and discard half of the water.

Use your hands to break off a chunk of cheese slightly larger than a golf ball and stretch it into a 12-inch rope (initially, you may want to dip your hands in a bowl of cold water to work with the hot cheese). Fold it in half onto itself, then stretch it and fold it again three more times, until the cheese becomes a lot stiffer. Shred the cheese into strands and add them to the bowl of cold cream. Repeat the process until all the cheese strands are in the bowl. Stir to combine until most of the cream has been absorbed. Store the stracciatella in an airtight container in the fridge for up to 4 days.

Ricotta

MAKES ABOUT 1 CUP

Just like mayonnaise, ricotta is the kind of thing that once you know how to make it yourself, you'll wonder why you ever bothered buying it from a store. Its uses are numerous—stuff it in pasta, layer a lasagna with it or spread it on toast for breakfast while it's still warm with a poached egg or a side of jam.

Make cheese curds: In a heavy-bottomed pot, heat the milk on medium-low heat until it starts to steam but just before it begins to boil, about 10–12 minutes. If you're using a thermometer, it should read 191°F.

Remove the milk from the heat and add 3 tbsp lemon juice, stirring quickly using a metal spoon. You should notice the milk "breaking," meaning that the curds and the whey have started to separate. If that's not happening, add more lemon juice, stir and give it a little more time. Cover the pot and let the curds and whey rest for about 5 minutes.

Strain the curds: Set up a fine-mesh strainer lined with cheesecloth over a large bowl or large, tall container. Using a slotted spoon, gently transfer the larger curds from the milk pot into the strainer, then transfer those strained curds temporarily into a small bowl and set aside. Pick up the pot and slowly pour the whey and any remaining curds through the strainer. The leftover whey can be discarded or used as a base for the Meatballs (p. 185). Return the larger curds to the strainer and let the cheese drain fully, about 1 hour. The final ricotta should be somewhat firm to the touch. Store in the fridge for up to 3 days.

Special Equipment
Instant-read thermometer
Cheesecloth

4 cups whole milk
3–5 tbsp fresh lemon juice

Mascarpone

MAKES 3 CUPS

Special Equipment
Instant-read thermometer
Cheesecloth

4 cups 35% cream
1 tbsp fresh lemon juice

Store-bought mascarpone can be extremely expensive, but what a lot of people don't realize is just how easy it is to make at home. It's also very versatile. Use it to replace ricotta in your next stuffed pasta project, add a dollop to your polenta to make it extra creamy or add a bit of sugar and serve it with our Chestnut Chocolate Cake (p. 239).

Cook the cream: In a medium pot, heat the cream over medium heat until it reaches 185°F. Remove from the heat and use a thermometer to measure the temperature as it lowers down to 140°F. Put the pot back on the burner and heat the cream over medium heat back up to 185°F. Maintain the temperature, add the lemon juice and whisk to combine. Cool the cream mixture back down to 140°F and store in an airtight container in the fridge overnight.

Strain the mascarpone: The following day, set a cheesecloth-lined strainer over a large bowl. Transfer the mascarpone mixture to the strainer and let it drain in the fridge for at least 12 hours. The mascarpone will keep in the fridge for 1 week.

Taleggio Fonduta

MAKES 4 CUPS

1 tbsp unsalted butter
1 small white onion, sliced
1½ tbsp all-purpose flour
1 clove garlic, crushed
1 bay leaf
1 clove
¼ whole nutmeg, finely grated
4 sprigs fresh thyme
2 tbsp dry porcini
1 tsp black peppercorns
Kosher salt
4 cups 35% cream
¼ lb (113 g) taleggio, cut into 2-inch cubes

This serves as the base for our Mr. Fun-Guy pizza (p. 94), but it can easily stand in for a creamy mushroom pasta sauce or a decadent sauce for a side of roasted potatoes.

Cook the cream: Heat a frying pan over medium heat. Add the butter and onions and sweat until translucent, about 5 minutes. Add the flour, garlic, bay leaf, clove, nutmeg, thyme, porcini, peppercorns and salt. Stir and cook until the flour is golden, lowering the heat when necessary to avoid burning. Whisk in the cream and bring to a simmer, then reduce the heat and cook on low for 30 minutes.

Make the fonduta: Strain the cream mixture into a medium bowl using a fine-mesh strainer. Add the taleggio cubes to the bowl while the mixture is still hot, whisking to melt and combine. Set aside to cool. Store in the fridge for up to 1 week.

Parmesan Stock

MAKES 4 CUPS

2 cups or more parmesan rinds
5–6 cups water
1 large onion, roughly chopped
1 medium carrot, peeled and roughly chopped
1 stalk celery, roughly chopped
½ leek, roughly chopped
1 head garlic, cut in half
4 sprigs fresh thyme
3 bay leaves
10 black peppercorns

We use an incredible amount of parmesan at the restaurant every week, and throwing out the rinds is out of the question (again, not a rule, but potentially a crime). Instead, we use them to make parmesan stock. It's delicious on its own as a vegetarian broth and it works wonders when cooking rice or blanching vegetables. It will truly bring your cooking to the next level.

Make the stock: In a medium pot, combine all the ingredients and bring to a simmer over medium-high heat. Reduce the heat to low and cook, covered, for 1½ hours. Strain the stock and use it to make Suppli (p. 151) or to blanch vegetables. Store in the fridge for a week or keep in the freezer for a few months.

Creamy Polenta

SERVES 4–6

3 cups whole milk (or more to loosen)

3 cups water

1 cup polenta (coarse cornmeal)

1½ cups finely grated parmesan

4 tbsp unsalted butter

3 tsp kosher salt

This polenta is great to accompany hearty meat dishes like Lamb Osso Bucco with Saffron Threads (p. 189) or Meatballs (p. 185), but it's also great for breakfast topped with a soft poached egg and a drizzle of Chris's Crispy Chili Oil (p. 256). Our creamy polenta is very rich, but you can easily make it lighter by replacing some of the milk with water and reducing the amount of cheese and butter.

Make the polenta: In a medium pot, bring the milk and water to a boil over medium-high heat. Reduce the heat to medium. Gradually add the polenta to the pot, whisking constantly, and bring to a simmer. Reduce the heat to low and cover the pot. Continue cooking, whisking every 10–15 minutes, until the polenta has thickened and is no longer gritty, about 30–35 minutes. Remove from the heat and add the parmesan, butter and salt. Whisk until the butter and cheese have melted and the polenta is the consistency of porridge, about 1 minute. Serve with lamb (p. 189) or meatballs in tomato sauce (p. 255). The polenta can be made up to 3 hours ahead. Simply store, covered, at room temperature and reheat over medium-low, adding milk as needed to loosen.

Garlic Butter

MAKES ½ CUP

This is a very simple and straightforward garlic butter recipe. Feel free to put it on literally everything or freeze it for later use.

Make the garlic butter: In a small pot, melt the butter and garlic together over low heat. Simmer until the butter becomes very fragrant, keeping the temperature very low and stirring occasionally to make sure the garlic doesn't burn, about 10 minutes. Remove from the heat, add the parsley and salt, and stir to combine. Let the butter cool down and firm up a little before serving. The garlic butter will keep in an airtight container in the fridge for up to 1 week.

¼ lb (113 g) unsalted butter

3 cloves garlic, finely chopped or Microplaned

1 tbsp chopped fresh parsley

½ tsp kosher salt

PICKLES

Pickling Vegetables

The next few recipes outline various techniques we use for pickling and preserving vegetables. This first one is our basic technique to make beautiful pickles that will last for a couple of months in the fridge. We usually make a large batch of this pickle brine and keep it in the fridge in case we stumble upon a beautiful vegetable bounty at the market and want to make them last a little longer. Feel free to add aromatics like garlic, coriander seeds, thyme and dried chili flakes to your pickles when packing them in the jars for some extra flavor.

Prepare your vegetables: There are no clear-cut rules, but we prefer to slice shallots, onions, celery, cucumbers, fennel and summer squashes. We trim, peel or wedge (depending on the type and size) carrots, cauliflower, radishes and wax beans.

Pick your seasonings: Feel free to try different things here, but usually garlic goes a long way, while herbs and spices like mustard seeds, dried chili flakes, coriander seeds, peppercorns, thyme sprigs and rosemary sprigs do a great job at infusing your vegetables with extra flavor.

Choose between hot or cold brine: Most vegetables do fantastic in a cold brine, while some benefit from a hot brine. We suggest using a cold brine for shallots, onions, cauliflower, celery, cucumbers, fennel, wax beans, summer squashes and radishes, and a hot brine for fresh chilies, asparagus and ramps.

(continued)

1 lb (450 g) vegetables of your choice
A few sprigs or ½ tsp seasonings of your choice

Basic Pickling Brine
1½ cups white wine vinegar
½ cup water
⅓ cup granulated sugar
2½ tsp kosher salt

(Pickling Vegetables continued)

Make the brine: Put all the brine ingredients in a pot (for hot brine) or a large jar (for cold brine) and stir until the sugar and salt have dissolved. If you're making hot brine pickles, bring the brine to a boil before packing your vegetables.

Pickle the vegetables: Pack your vegetables and desired seasonings and aromatics into clean mason jars. Pour your cold or hot brine over the vegetables until they are fully submerged, and screw on the lid. (If you're using hot brine, let the jar cool before refrigerating.) You can start eating them as soon as you want, but the flavors will be more developed after a week or so. They will keep in the fridge for up to 2 months and are a great addition to spruce up any crudité plate (see Pinzimonio on p. 25) or to add some zing to a hoagie.

Pickled Shallots

MAKES 1 CUP

3 medium shallots
¼ cup white wine vinegar
¼ cup red wine vinegar
3 tbsp water
2 tsp sugar
1 tsp kosher salt

This easy and quick pickling process takes the edge off the shallots' raw onion taste, making them the perfect addition to your summer salads. The pickling liquid is just as good and versatile as the shallots themselves and can be used to replace the base vinegar in many dressing recipes.

Prepare the shallots: Depending on the recipe you are making, either slice the shallots into thin rings or cut them into medium-size dice. Pack in a mason jar and set aside.

Mix the liquid and pickle the shallots: In a small bowl, combine the white wine vinegar, red wine vinegar, water, sugar and salt. Stir until the salt and sugar have completely dissolved. Pour the liquid over the shallots, making sure they are fully submerged. You can use the shallots as soon as you want, but we recommend waiting at least 20 minutes (the longer you wait, the more the flavors will develop). The pickled shallots will keep for up to 1 month in the fridge.

Giardiniera

MAKES 8½ CUPS (ABOUT FOUR 16 OZ/500 ML JARS)

Our friend and pizza genius Chris Cameron is obsessed with all things pickled. This recipe is his baby. It's a great way to preserve the best summer vegetables and enjoy them year-round. This is addictive on a hoagie, and in a pinch, you can swap it in for the honey mushrooms in the Dante Salad (p. 30).

Prepare the vegetables: In a very large heatproof bowl, combine the beans, cauliflower, sweet and spicy peppers, onions, celery, carrots and garlic. Add 12 cups water.

Brine the vegetables: In a small pot, combine 4 cups water and the kosher salt. Bring to a boil, whisking until the salt has dissolved. Remove from the heat and add the ice to cool down the brine. Pour the mixture into the bowl of soaking vegetables, stirring lightly to distribute evenly. Cover with a plate and top with a heavy object (like a can) to weigh the vegetables down. Place in the fridge for at least 12 hours.

Drain the vegetables: Use a strainer to drain the vegetables, reserving 1 cup cold brine, and transfer to a large bowl. Nestle the dill fronds and stems with the vegetables.

Make the pickling liquid: In a medium pot, combine the bay leaves, peppercorns, mustard seeds, coriander seeds, celery seeds, fennel seeds, oregano, sugar, vinegar, 1 cup reserved brine and olive oil. Bring to a simmer and immediately turn off the heat. Pour the hot pickling liquid over the vegetables and let it rest until it has completely cooled down.

Pack the giardiniera: Using a slotted spoon, transfer the vegetables to the jars and fill with pickling liquid until they are fully submerged. The flavors will be fully developed after 1 week, but you can start tasting after a few days to see how it's going. The giardiniera will keep in the fridge for up to 1 year (as long as the vegetables are fully submerged).

Vegetables + Brine

½ lb (225 g) green beans, trimmed and cut into 1-inch pieces

½ medium head cauliflower or Romanesco, cut into 1-inch florets

1½ sweet peppers (bell, Hungarian or Cubanelle), cut into 1-inch strips

½ spicy pepper (jalapeno, banana or red hot), thinly sliced

3 cipollini onions or ½ medium white onion, cut into 6, petals separated

1 stalk celery, cut into 1-inch cubes

2 small carrots, peeled and cut into ½-inch rounds

3 cloves garlic, quartered

16 cups water, divided

1½ cups kosher salt

2 cups ice

1 handful fresh dill fronds and stems

Pickling Liquid

2 bay leaves

1 tbsp black peppercorns

1 tbsp mustard seeds

1 tbsp coriander seeds

1 tbsp celery seeds

1 tbsp fennel seeds

1 tbsp dried oregano

2 tbsp + 2 tsp sugar

3 cups white wine vinegar

1 cup reserved cold brine

½ cup extra virgin olive oil

Pickled Honey Mushrooms

MAKES 2 CUPS

Cute and delightful. This method will work with just about any mushrooms (you might just need to adjust the cooking time). We add them to the Porchetta and Sage hoagie (p. 215) and the Dante Salad (p. 30), but you can top and brighten up just about any meat dish with these mushrooms.

Make the pickled mushrooms: In a frying pan, heat half of the olive oil on high heat. Add the garlic, thyme and bay leaf and cook until fragrant. Add the mushrooms and sear slightly, for about 10 seconds, then deglaze the pan with the sherry vinegar and continue cooking until the liquids have reduced by half, about 15 more seconds. Remove from the heat, season to taste with salt and pepper and add the remaining olive oil. Set aside to cool. The mushrooms can be stored in the fridge for up to 2 weeks.

½ cup extra virgin olive oil, divided

2 cloves garlic, smashed

4 sprigs fresh thyme

1 bay leaf

4 cups honey (shimeji) mushrooms (one 5.2 oz/150 g package)

4 tbsp sherry vinegar

½ tsp kosher salt

Pinch freshly ground black pepper

Marinated Artichokes

MAKES 3 CUPS

3 lemons, cut in half

5 very large or 10 small artichokes

⅓ cup extra virgin olive oil

1–2 cloves garlic, sliced

1 small onion, cut into thick slices

1 medium carrot, peeled and finely sliced

1 large or 2 small tomatoes, roughly chopped

A few sprigs fresh thyme

2 cups white wine

¼ cup white wine vinegar

2 tbsp kosher salt

Freshly ground black pepper

We love adding marinated artichokes to anything, from salads to pasta. We just think that artichokes are incredibly special vegetables. So special, in fact, that their plants even produce different-size chokes, which means you might find different-size artichokes coming from the same plant at the same time of year. Here, we explain how to turn an artichoke to extract its heart, but if you really want to be truly impressed, look up videos of Jacques Pépin's technique and learn from the master.

Make the lemon water: Fill a large bowl with water. Squeeze the lemons into it, then drop them in the bowl.

Prepare the artichokes: Starting from the stem, pull and snap off the tougher outer leaves of an artichoke, working your way around the artichoke until you reach the pale inner leaves (you will be discarding quite a few leaves!). Trim the stem to about 2 inches long and peel it, using a small paring knife, to remove the fibrous outer layer, leaving only the sweet and tender core of the stem.

Next, use a paring knife to sculpt the base of the artichoke, removing any leaf ends or dark green bits, until you reveal the pale inner layer and achieve a nice round shape to the base, following the natural shape of the artichoke so that you remove only the inedible part.

With a larger knife, cut off and discard (or compost) the top half of the artichoke leaves. Then cut the artichoke in half lengthwise to reveal the center choke. Using a small spoon or a melon baller, scoop out the hairy part of the choke and the small fibers attached to the base: the tender inner leaves, the base (known as the heart) and the stem are the only edible parts of the artichoke. Put the prepared artichoke in the lemon water and repeat the process with the remaining artichokes.

Cook the artichokes: In a Dutch oven, heat the olive oil over medium-high heat. Drain and pat dry the artichokes. When the oil is very hot and close to smoking, gently add the artichokes, being careful not to splash any hot oil on yourself. You should hear a dramatic sizzle.

Using a wooden spoon, stir the artichokes around until they gain some color, 3–5 minutes. Add the garlic, onions, carrots, tomatoes and thyme and cook until the ingredients are hot, about 2 minutes. Add the white wine, wine vinegar, salt and pepper and bring to a simmer. Make sure there is enough liquid in the pot to cover the artichokes. Add up to ½ cup water if needed. Bring everything to a simmer, then cover the pot and reduce the heat to a minimum. Cook until the artichokes are just tender but not at all mushy, 10 minutes for small and 15 minutes for large ones. Turn off the heat and let the artichokes cool down in the pot, covered, for 30 minutes.

Pack the artichokes: When the artichokes have fully absorbed the aromatics while cooling down, transfer them to a mason jar. Then use a fine-mesh sieve to strain the cooking liquid over them. Store in the fridge for up to 1 week.

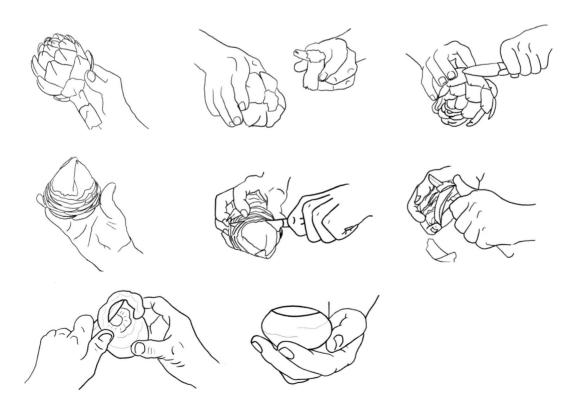

Pepperoncini

MAKES 2 CUPS (ABOUT ONE 16 OZ/500 ML JAR)

2 ⅓ cups sliced medium-heat chilies (roughly 12 red serrano or spicy Cherry Bomb peppers)

½ cup red wine vinegar

3 tsp sugar

2 tsp kosher salt

¾ cup extra virgin olive oil

½ cup diced onions

At the restaurant, we serve pepperoncini on the Diavolo 2.0 pizza (p. 87) and in the peach and pistachio salad (p. 37), but at home, we put this stuff on everything. It's especially good in a sandwich to balance out the richness of certain meats and cheeses. Use this method to transform and preserve any kind of chilies or peppers you might encounter—and don't be afraid to mix and match.

Brine the chilies: In a large bowl, stir to combine the sliced chilies, vinegar, sugar and salt. Cover and leave to rest for at least 8 hours (or overnight) at room temperature.

Make the pepperoncini: In a frying pan, heat the olive oil over medium. Add the onions and cook until they start to sweat and become translucent, about 5 minutes. Remove from the heat. Add the chilies and their juices to the onion mixture and cook 5 more minutes. Cool slightly, then transfer to a clean mason jar to cool completely. Store in the fridge for up to 2 months.

Bread and Butter Pickles

MAKES 10 CUPS (ABOUT FIVE 16 OZ/500 ML JARS)

This is Chris's family recipe, which he has perfected over the years. It does an incredible job at elevating and transforming a humble tomato hoagie (p. 211) into one of the best sandwiches we've ever had.

Make the salt brine: In a small pot, combine 1 cup water and the salt. Bring to a boil and whisk until the salt has dissolved. Turn off the heat. Add 1 cup cold water and let cool completely.

Brine the cucumbers: In a large bowl, combine the cucumbers with the salt brine. Add the ice, cover with a plate and top with a heavy object (a can of tomatoes works well) to weigh down the cucumbers and make sure they stay submerged. Store in the fridge overnight.

Make the pickles: The next day, drain the cucumbers out of the salt brine. Discard the salty water. In a large heatproof container or bowl, combine the cucumbers with the sliced onions and garlic. In a small pot, combine the white vinegar, apple cider vinegar, sugar, celery seeds, mustard seeds, allspice berries and turmeric, whisking to combine until the sugar is dissolved. Bring to a boil. Pour the hot brine over the vegetables. Let the mixture cool to room temperature, then transfer to mason jars. Cover and close the jars. Store in the fridge for up to 1 month.

Salt Brine

2 cups water, divided

¼ cup kosher salt

Bread and Butter Pickles

2½ lb (1.1 kg) cucumbers (Kirby is ideal), sliced

2 cups ice

1 small onion, sliced

2 cloves garlic, thinly sliced

1¾ cups white vinegar

1¾ cups apple cider vinegar

2½ cups light brown sugar or 1¼ cups each granulated and dark brown sugar

1 tbsp celery seeds

1 tbsp mustard seeds

1 tsp whole allspice berries

1 tsp turmeric powder

THANK YOU

First of all, thank you to all of our staff for helping us become who we are and for always inspiring us. *Salad Pizza Wine* would have never been possible without your hard work. To our partner Emma Cardarelli, thank you for trusting we would do Elena justice with this book.

Thank you to Michelle Marek for sharing your desserts and gracing us with your patience and insights while testing and developing our recipes. Thank you Kendra McKnight for imparting your recipe-testing and writing advice to us. Thanks to Chris Cameron, our pizza guru, without whose guidance we would certainly be lost. Your passion and attention to detail is second to none. To Willow Cardinal, a huge thank you for your help creating recipes and showing up at the crack of dawn to prepare food for photo shoots.

Thank you to Dominique Lafond, who has been taking photos of all of us at Elena since before we even opened our doors. You have been and always will be part of the Elena family. Thanks to our photo stylist, Élisabeth Racine, for your impeccable taste and talent for finding unusual pieces. To Emilie Campbell, thank you for not batting an eye when we asked you to draw a bunch of snakes in costumes for a cookbook.

Thank you to Maison Sévigny, Verre d'Onge, Jo Rassi, Xenia Taler, and Mepra for lending us your beautiful pieces to highlight our food. To our friends and family: Pauline, Juliette, and Napoléon Mercier; Fraser Ballard and Alex Lafleur; Nathan Fournier; Emily Eisen; Marie-Pier Pigeon, and to Eva and Maria Gracia Turgeon, thank you for letting us borrow your plates, glasses, and tablecloths. Thanks to Jesse Massumi and Jesse Mulder at Pumpui for the beers. Thanks to Maxim Turcotte for keeping us warm in North Face. Thanks to Ooni for the pizza oven—it's the closest we've ever got to recreating our pizzas at home.

Thank you to Michel Morand, Johanne Laporte, and Dominique L. Massé for allowing us to shoot at your cottage in the middle of a pandemic. Thanks to Joanna Kolb, Matthew Morein, and Mosi Morein for your friendship and for welcoming us into your backyard for our last photo

shoot (we're really sorry we set your bathroom on fire). Thank you to Mackenzie Aker, Laurie-Anne Beaulieu, Rachel Buchanan, Kyle Calma, Valérie Chagnon, Marcus Granada, Sloane Etta Gray, Julio Mendy, Philippe Minkoué, Ashley Olivieri, Jarred Reed-Stewart, Andrew Sayo, and to everyone else who posed for the photos in this book, for looking so good.

Thank you to our agent, Kimberly Witherspoon, and to Maria Whelan for first believing in the idea for this book and for your constant support. To the Appetite by Random House team—our editor, Lindsay Paterson; publisher, Robert McCullough; book designer, Jennifer Griffiths; copy editor, Lana Okerlund; and publishing assistant, Colin Rier—thank you for understanding and capturing us so perfectly.

Janice would like to thank: Ryan, Marley, and Emma, for your confidence in me. Thank you to the entire Elena staff, past and present. Steph, thank you for your patience, humor and herbal teas! Thanks to all the farms and suppliers we work with who bring us exquisite ingredients, without which there would be no inspiration. Thank you to Kendra McKnight and Joost for listening to me for hours and believing in me. Thank you to my family for being as obsessed with food as I am, and for encouraging me in everything I do.

Stephanie would like to thank: Ryan, Marley and Emma for trusting me with putting our story at Elena into words—dumb jokes, sad bits and all. Thank you to Janice for spending countless afternoons writing recipes with me and making me laugh through it all. Thank you to Rachel and Emilie for being the two best friends I could have ever asked for, and for always encouraging me. Thank you to Joanna Fox for

your priceless advice. Thank you to my family for always supporting me even if you don't always understand what I do for work.

Ryan would like to thank: Steph for bringing this book to life and for capturing Elena as only you could have. I'm so proud of you. Janice for your tireless commitment, brilliant recipes and for always making sure I'm well fed. Marley and Emma, you grew our little restaurant into such an incredible business—I'm forever grateful and humbled to be your partner. Thank you, Rachel, for your endless support; I could not have done any of this without you. Sloane, thank you for being the best thing that's ever happened to me. Mom and dad for always believing in me. Thank you to everyone who helped make Elena the special place it is.

Marley would like to thank: Steph for dreaming up this cookbook as soon as we opened Elena, at a time when we had no business doing so. Genius? Janice for your resolved commitment to all of our harebrained challenges. Emma and Ryan for your faith in me and giving me the space and patience to grow up. Mom, Kay and Dad for inspiring a love of hosting. Cass for teaching me even when I didn't want to be taught. Lev for mostly always being on board nearly all of the time. Natasha2 for being my sounding board and very partial party.

INDEX